JUN - - 2016

J947 TORCHINSKII
TorchinskiÄ-, O
Russia /

P9-CJZ-920

CULTURES OF THE WORLD
Russia

Alameda Free Library
1550 Oak Street
Alameda, CA 94501

Cavendish
Square
New York

Published in 2016 by Cavendish Square Publishing, LLC
243 5th Avenue, Suite 136, New York, NY 10016
Copyright © 2016 by Cavendish Square Publishing, LLC
First Edition

No part of this publication may be reproduced, stored in a retrieval system, or transmitted in any form or by any means—electronic, mechanical, photocopying, recording, or otherwise—without the prior permission of the copyright owner. Request for permission should be addressed to Permissions, Cavendish Square Publishing, 243 5th Avenue, Suite 136, New York, NY 10016. Tel (877) 980-4450; fax (877) 980-4454.

Website: cavendishsq.com

This publication represents the opinions and views of the author based on his or her personal experience, knowledge, and research. The information in this book serves as a general guide only. The author and publisher have used their best efforts in preparing this book and disclaim liability rising directly or indirectly from the use and application of this book.

CPSIA Compliance Information: Batch #WS15CSQ
All websites were available and accurate when this book was sent to press.

Cataloging-in-Publication Data
Torchinsky, Oleg.
Russia / by Oleg Torchinsky, Angela Black, and Debbie Nevins.
p. cm. — (Cultures of the world)
Includes index.
ISBN 978-1-50260-342-5 (hardcover) ISBN 978-1-50260-343-2 (ebook)
1. Russia (Federation) — Juvenile literature. I. Torchinskiĭ, O. (Oleg) II. Title.
DK510.23 T67 2016
947—d23

Writers, Oleg Torchinsky; Angela Black, third edition
Editorial Director, third edition: David McNamara
Editor, third edition: Debbie Nevins
Art Director, third edition: Jeffrey Talbot
Designer, third edition: Jessica Nevins
Production Manager, third edition Jennifer Ryder-Talbot
Picture Researcher, third edition: Jessica Nevins

PICTURE CREDITS

The photographs in this book are used with the permission of: Mordolff/Getty Images, cover; OlegDoroshin/Shutterstock.com 1; fototehnik/Shutterstock.com, 3; Sergei Kazakov/Shutterstock.com, 5; forden/Shutterstock.com, 6; Andrey Burmakin/Shutterstock.com, 7; Andrey Rudakov/Bloomberg/Getty Images, 8; Helen Filatova/Shutterstock.com, 9; Vladimir Melnikov/Shutterstock.com, 10; Anna Maksimyuk/Shutterstock.com, 12; Oleg Gekman/Shutterstock.com, 13; Martynova Anna/Shutterstock.com, 14; Dean Conger/National Geographic/Getty Images, 15; Eduard Kyslynskyy/Shutterstock.com, 16; Dvorko Sergey/Shutterstock.com, 17; Pavel Burchenko/Shutterstock.com, 18; Olgysha/Shutterstock.com, 19; Valeri Potapova/Shutterstock.com, 20; Lilyana Vynogradova/Shutterstock.com, 21; Sovfoto/UIG/Getty Images, 22; www.picture.art-catalog.ru/picture.php?id_picture=3335/File:Vasnetsov Bapt Vladimir.jpg/Wikimedia Commons, 24; Apollinari Vasnetsov (1864-1933)/File:Moscow daniel.jpg/Wikimedia Commons, 25; Nikolay Shustov, 1860/File:Nikolay Shustov 001.jpg/Wikimedia Commons, 27; Nikolay Sauerweid/File:ZauerveydNA Petr1UsmirDA19.jpg/Wikimedia Commons, 28; Fyodor Rokotov/ile:Profile portrait of Catherine II by Fedor Rokotov (1763, Tretyakov gallery).jpg/Wikimedia Commons, 29; Thesupermat/File:Au service des Tsars - inv. P-2379 - Attaque du carré des décabristes par le régiment des gardes à cheval le 14 décembre 1825.jpg/Wikimedia Commons, 30; Nikolai Vasilyevich Nevrev/File:NEVREV Torg.jpg/Wikimedia Commons, 32; Boissonnas & Eggler/File:Nicholas II by Boissonnas & Eggler c1909.jpg/Wikimedia Commons, 33; Buyenlarge/Getty Images, 34; Laski Diffusion/Getty Images, 35; Hulton Archive/Getty Images, 38; Vladimír Tóth/File:DNV opona.jpg/Wikimedia Commons, 40; Eamonn McCormack/Getty Images, 41; Fine Art Images/Heritage Images/Getty Images, 42; Sovfoto/UIG/Getty Images, 42; Drop of Light/Shutterstock.com, 43; Alexsey Druginyn/AFP/Getty Images, 44; Ekaterina Bykova/Shutterstock.com, 46, vvoc/Shutterstock.com, 48; Andromed/Shutterstock.com, 49; Sergei Butorin/Shutterstock.com, 50; FABRICE COFFRINI/AFP/Getty Images, 51; The Asahi Shimbun/Getty Images, 52; Alexis DUCLOS/Gamma-Rapho/Getty Images, 54; Sovfoto/UIG/Getty Images, 55; Lonely Planet/Lonely Planet Images/Getty Images, 58; ALEXANDER NEMENOV/AFP/Getty Images, 60; SERGEY KULIKOV/AFP/Getty Images, 61; Dmitry Beliakov/Bloomberg/Getty Images, 62; withGod/Shutterstock.com, 63; Richard Whitcombe/Shutterstock.com, 64; Joymsk140/Shutterstock.com, 65; Svetlana Arapova/Shutterstock.com, 66; withGod/Shutterstock.com, 69; PhotoPrince/Shutterstock.com, 70; Universal History Archive/UIG/Getty Images, 71; Maryna Kulchytska/Shutterstock.com, 72; Iakov Filimonov/Shutterstock.com, 74; Svetlana Arapova/Shutterstock.com, 75; Grigvovan/Shutterstock.com, 76; Martynova Anna/Shutterstock.com, 77; Maria Sbytova/Shutterstock.com 78; Alex Alekseev/Shutterstock.com, 79; abadesign/Shutterstock.com, 80; Alexey U/Shutterstock.com, 81; ALEXANDER NEMENOV/AFP/Getty Images, 82; ID1974/Shutterstock.com, 83; Anonymous/File:Doloy prazdniki.jpg/Wikimedia Commons, 84; Mikhail Pogosov/Shutterstock.com, 86; Irina Papoyan/Shutterstock.com, 87; Angelina Dimitrova/Shutterstock.com, 88; vvoronov/Shutterstock.com, 90; De Visu/Shutterstock.com, 91; Fine Art Images/Heritage Images/Getty Images, 92; Andrey Rudakov/Bloomberg/Getty Image, 93; Iakov Filimonov/Shutterstock.com, 94; Popperfoto/Getty Images, 96; irisphoto1/Shutterstock.com, 97; vvoe/Shutterstock.com, 98; Fine Art Images/Heritage Images/Getty Images, 99; dimbar76/Shutterstock.com, 100; AlexSoft, 2004/File:Apotheosis.jpg/Wikimedia Commons, 101; 1907/File:Natalia Goncharova (self-portrait, 1907, GTG).jpg/Wikimedia Commons, 102; Sovfoto/UIG/Getty Images, 103; Pavel L Photo and Video/Shutterstock.com, 105; Rob Kim/Getty Images, 106; Laski Collection/Getty Images, 107; Trofimov Denis/Shutterstock.com, 110; Walenrod/Shutterstock.com, 111; My Good Images/Shutterstock.com, 112; Makushin Alexey/Shutterstock.com, 113; Lipskiy/Shutterstock.com, 114; Pavel L Photo and Video/Shutterstock.com, 115; withGod/Shutterstock.com, 116; ID1974/Shutterstock.com, 118; Alexey Borodin/Shutterstock.com, 119; Vladimir V. Georgievskiy/Shutterstock.com, 120; Amos Chapple/Lonely Planet Images/Getty Images, 122; Alex Kosev/Shutterstock.com, 123; Pressmaster/Shutterstock.com, 124; elenamych/Shutterstock.com, 126; Sovfoto/UIG/Getty Images, 127; Africa Studio/Shutterstock.com, 128; minadezhda/Shutterstock.com, 130; Iryna Melnyk/Shutterstock.com, 131.

PRECEDING PAGE

St. Basil's Cathedral in Moscow is perhaps the most iconic image of Russia.

Printed in the United States of America

CONTENTS

RUSSIA TODAY

THE CONDITION OF RUSSIA TODAY IS COMPLEX, CHANGING, and—for many neighboring countries—alarming. Russia seems to be flexing its military muscle and looking to regain the great power status it had when it was the largest country inside the Soviet Union (USSR, 1922—1991). In 2008, Russian President Vladimir Putin sent troops into neighboring Georgia (also once a part of the Soviet Union) in response to a conflict over two small regions with strong ties to Russia. The international community was outraged, but did little.

In 2014, the Crimea Peninsula, part of Ukraine, became the focus of the worst East-West crisis since the Cold War (1945—1990). After Ukraine's president was driven from power, pro-Russian forces seized Crimea. They then voted in an election, declared illegal by Ukraine, to make Crimea part of Russia. In eastern Ukraine pro-Russian rebels aided by Russian military equipment, and supported by Russia, have been fighting the Ukrainian army to establish an independent territory. This has sent shivers all over Eastern Europe, especially among countries that used to be, like Russia, part of the Soviet Union.

Putin's increasingly authoritarian rule, his desire to reconstruct Russian power through authoritarian rule and his crackdown on domestic critics led some to call him "Czar Vladimir," linking him to Russia's imperial rulers of the past. Putin has modernized and strengthened Russia's armed forces. He has ended the rule of oligarchs, the multibillionaires who controlled much of the Russian economy. Under Putin's rule, Russia has entered a new period of prosperity fueled by the country's vast reserves of oil and natural gas. Russia is now the world's number one oil-producing nation. Oil and other natural resources from Russia's vast storehouse have fueled a growing economy that is still trying to throw off the shackles of the inefficient communist economy that had crippled Russian industry since the 1920s and 1930s.

Russia has a new middle class that is very similar to the middle class in both Europe and the United States. Like most middle class people, Russia's middle class is concerned with material prosperity and stability. People who have not been to Russia in years often remark about how much the big cities of Moscow and St. Petersburg have changed with the introduction of US-based fast-food restaurants, Western banks, international apparel

A McDonald's in St. Petersburg is just one of the many Western fast-food places in Russia.

stores, new office buildings and other structures that show off Russia's middle class consumer culture. Outside of Russia's major urban areas, however, change has been slow. Some villages look little different than they did in the 1950s under Soviet rule. One of the major conflicts in coming years will be the divide between "new Russia" and "old Russia."

Economic growth, however, has led to air, ground, and water pollution in Russia, especially in mining and industrial areas. Russia under Soviet rule had already been polluted by the rapid growth of heavy industry. Many plant and animal species are threatened, but the Russian government is beginning to take strong measures to protect the land's natural heritage.

Young Russians listen intently to their president in February 2015.

Inside Russia, Putin has now fully established government control over the media. A vast majority of Russians still get most of their information from television, and the three major channels are either owned directly by the government or by government-owned companies. Major newspapers have been intimidated. Russia's only independent television channel—TV Rain—is facing enormous pressure to shut down. More recently, Putin has cracked down against gay people and passed a number of laws forbidding what Putin calls "gay propaganda." He has even imprisoned members of an all-female rock group that sang anti-Putin songs.

PUTIN'S POPULARITY

While Putin's repressive measures have made him unpopular in the West, many Russians see Putin as a strong leader who has begun to restore Russia to its past greatness as a major world power. Polls taken in late 2014 show

An employee poses with a Putin T-shirt from the Patriot collection inside an Alexander Konasov clothing store in Moscow,

that 87 percent of the Russian people support Putin and his policies—an astounding figure that no American president has ever come close to. (President Barack Obama's favorability rating hovered at around 40 percent in December 2014.) Putin's popularity draws on a long tradition in Russia of supporting strong rulers who can get things done.

That said, Putin's reputation did take a hit in early 2015 when his chief political rival, and one of his most outspoken critics, was murdered. On February 28, Boris Nemtsov, 55, a former deputy prime minister, was shot four times from a passing car as he was walking just outside the Kremlin. Many Russians suspected Putin of being behind the killing, though others disagreed. Nemtsov was not the first Putin critic to end up dead.

Much of Putin's popularity draws support from nostalgia for Russia's recent history. During the Cold War, the Soviet Union was a superpower vying for world influence with the world's other superpower, the United States. During that time, life inside the USSR was relatively stable. Everyone knew his or her own place in the Soviet dictatorship. In 1991, however, the Soviet Union collapsed and dissolved into fifteen independent countries, among them Russia itself and Ukraine. Russia officially became a democracy, but its economy fell apart. Poverty, crime, lawlessness seemed to rule the land. By 2000, when Putin began his first term as president, things seemed to have gotten even worse. He pledged to change things on two fronts. His foreign policy, he said, was to regain Russia's place in world affairs. His domestic policy was to restore stability, to end what he called "revolutions" that had brought Russia low. These two core objectives have inspired everything that Putin has done since.

Red Square in Moscow is a national landmark and a popular tourist destination.

ECONOMIC CRISIS

Putin's push to strengthen Russia, however, has recently run into an economic roadblock. World oil prices hit a five-year low in January 2015. Since oil makes up about 60 percent of Russia's exports, Russia now has less money to spend on its military and on other projects. The Russian ruble went down 40 percent against the dollar by the end of 2014. That means that imported products became more expensive for Russians to buy. Also, inflation was due to rise 9 percent in 2015 and to continue climbing. On December 2, 2014 the government predicted that Russia's already battered economy would fall into recession (negative economic growth) by the end of 2015.

Experts are unsure how Russia's economic situation will impact Putin's political agenda. Some analysts predict that Putin may feel compelled to temper his aggressive foreign policy and anti-Western stance in order to garner international sympathy and support. Others worry that "Czar Vladimir" may instead choose to encourage further upheaval abroad, similar to the unrest in Crimea, as a means of distracting the Russian people from their economic woes.

GEOGRAPHY

The Ob River in Siberia empties into the Gulf of Ob, and from there it flows into the Arctic Ocean.

1

T
HE ONE WORD THAT DESCRIBES Russia's geography is "vastness." The Russian Federation is the world's largest country in land area. East to West, it stretches from more than 5,600 miles (9,000 kilometers), from the Baltic Sea in Europe to within a few miles of Alaska. North to south, at its greatest width, Russia covers 2,500 miles (4,025 km). It spans two continents—Europe and Asia. Russia has erected a monument in the Ural Mountains where the border between Europe and Asia lies. Tourists like to be photographed there, standing with one foot in Europe and the other in Asia.

The Soviet Union covered an area of 8.65 million square miles (22.4 million square kilometers) and was the largest country on Earth in terms of area. Now that the Soviet Union no longer exists, Russia itself takes up 6.602 million square miles (17.1 million sq km)—and yet it is *still* the largest country on Earth.

PLAINS AND MOUNTAINS

Given its huge size, Russia possesses just about every type of geographical feature. If you travel east from the Belarus border, you will come upon flat plains that stretch eastward for thousands of miles. The westernmost part of Russia's plains are called the Russian, or East European Lowland. A little further are the Ural Mountains, which extend

Mount Elbrus dominates the view in the Caucasus Mountains.

around 1,600 miles (2,500 km) from the frigid waters of the Kara Sea to the arid plains of north Kazakhstan. The Urals are renowned for their mineral riches. Their highest peak is Mount Narodnaya, which is 6,217 feet (1,895 meters) high.

Once you leave the Urals on your eastward journey in Russia, you come upon another vast plain, the West Siberian Plain. Directly below the plains are the high peaks of the Caucasus Mountains, including Mount Elbrus, which at 18,481 feet (5,633 m), is Russia's highest mountain. Farther east is the Central Siberian Plateau, and if you travel still farther east you will pass through the mountain regions of eastern Siberia until you reach the Far East, China and Korea, and the Pacific Ocean.

Oceans wash Russia on the north, east, and west. In the north, Russia borders the Arctic Ocean, and in the east, the vast Pacific. In the west, Russia has an outlet on Europe's Baltic Sea, and from there, can access the Atlantic Ocean. Russia's ships can also reach the Mediterranean Sea through the Black Sea in the south.

RIVERS AND LAKES

Russia has many large rivers. One of the largest is the Volga River, which figures prominently in Russian history and folklore. Although the Volga is not Russia's longest river, there is no other river about which as many songs and books have been written. The Volga has been known since ancient times, when it was called the Ra; in the Middle Ages, it was known as the Itil. Beginning in the Valdei Hills northwest of Moscow as a tiny spring, the Volga flows south, becoming ever wider and stronger. After 2,193 miles (3,530 km) it forms a broad delta and flows into the Caspian Sea. A small chapel has been built at

the source of the Volga. More than 40 percent of Russia's people live near it and its tributaries and half of Russia's farmers live within reach of its banks.

The mighty Volga is Europe's longest river, but it cannot compete in length with the huge and powerful rivers of Siberia—the Ob, Lena, Yenisey, and Angara. They are each so wide that if you stand on one bank you cannot see the opposite side.

Lake Baikal in Siberia is surrounded by snow-topped mountains.

LAKE BAIKAL Among Russia's thousands of lakes, one is unique—Lake Baikal, the world's largest freshwater basin. At 5,315 feet (1,620 m) and twenty-five million years old, it is the deepest and oldest lake in the world. It is the habitat of a variety of flora and fauna (1,800 types), including some that are found nowhere else in the world. Another interesting feature distinguishes Baikal from other lakes: 336 rivers flow into the lake, while only one river flows out of it, the Angara River.

CLIMATE AND SEASONS

Due to its vast size, Russia has a variety of different climatic conditions, according to region and the time of year. In the northern arctic and subarctic zones, the average winter temperature is −58 degrees Fahrenheit (−50 degrees Celsius). By contrast, in the south and the Caucasus, summer temperatures can reach 110°F (43°C). Western Russia has a typical

Autumn in the mountains outside the city of Sochi, on the Black Sea, is a colorful season.

continental climate, with hot summers of up to 86°F (30°C) and cold winters as low as —13°F (—25°C).

In Russia, the four seasons of winter, spring, summer and autumn sharply differ from each other. The winter months of December, January, and February have frosts, ice, and snowstorms. During this season, the earth is blanketed in snow and ice. Before the winter comes, birds migrate to warmer lands, insects hide in the tree bark or go underground, and animals find shelter in dens and lairs.

Spring in western Russia begins in March and lasts through April and May. This is the time when the first flowers appear from under the snow; they are called snowdrops. The ice on the rivers begins to melt and break up, turning into rivulets of water. Rooks are the first birds to return from faraway countries, announcing the arrival of spring.

Spring is followed by the summer months: June, July, and August. Everything blooms; everything thrives and bears fruit.

Fall is considered the most beautiful time of the year in Russia. It is called "golden autumn," because the forest leaves turn golden-red. Particularly beautiful are the maple trees, whose leaves acquire a golden and bright-red tinge. In November, the trees shed their leaves, with only their bare branches outlined in black in the forest. Birds migrate southward to warmer lands, and animals hasten to hide in their warm dens.

FAUNA

An extremely large variety of animal, bird, reptile, and insect species live in Russia. Thousands of different fishes and marine animals inhabit its waters, and thousands of different plants and trees grow in its forests. The main animals inhabiting the forests of western Russia include the brown bear,

THE NORTH

The winter is particularly long in Russia's north, where the land is washed by the Arctic Ocean. Much of this region is almost perpetually ice-bound. Above this region of ice and eternal frost is the North Pole, which is not part of Russia.

The North Pole is not the coldest recorded spot on Earth, however. The coldest spot is a place called Oymyakon in Siberia. There, the temperature in winter may drop to –160°F (–106°C), a temperature that is hard to imagine. A bird that dares to fly out of its nest in such weather freezes and drops to the ground dead, frozen solid. On such days people stay home, and if they have to go outdoors, they wear clothes made of fur and cover their faces with special fur masks. They have to breathe through cloth or fur to prevent their lungs from freezing.

In the North, the winter lasts seven to eight months of the year. During this period it is dark and cold, with raging snowstorms and blizzards. The boundless tundra (vast, nearly treeless plains) is blanketed with snow; the bare forests and the cold empty plains are a terrible and unusual sight. Even so, there is a strange phenomenon reported by doctors and psychologists, who call this the "disease of the North." People who have spent some time in the North often want to return there. Neither the warm sea nor palm trees attract them; all they want is to go back to the cold regions of ice and snow.

One of the most magnificent sights in this part of the world is the Northern Lights. The effect of this strange phenomenon is as if someone were showing a color movie across the sky, with gold, white, silver, blue, pink, yellow, and red streamers and bands moving in ripples and illuminating the dark winter sky. This enchanting sight lasts one or two hours, gradually fading away until the sky sinks back into darkness. If you are lucky enough to see the Northern Lights, you will never forget the sight. The mechanism that causes this magnificent display is not fully understood, but it is connected with the proximity of the magnetic North Pole to high solar winds.

There are only about 350 adult Siberian tigers left in the world; 95 percent of them live in the far eastern part of Russia.

wolf, fox, hare, hedgehog, and polecat. The most common birds are the wood grouse, black grouse, partridge, hazel grouse, crow, magpie, and sparrow.

Other animals include the polar bear, which lives in the north among the snow and ice; the walrus; and the reindeer. Aurochs, a very ancient form of cattle dating back to the Ice Ages, nearly became extinct in recent times. It took conservationists much effort to find several animals and gradually revive the Russian herd. The Siberian taiga (TAI-gah) or subarctic forest, is also the habitat of sables; their fur is so beautiful and soft that it is often called "soft gold." In the far eastern taiga, there still roam a small number of Siberian tigers, which are an endangered species.

Russia's bird and insect species are much like those found in other regions of the world north of the equator. Many of the birds migrate to southern Asia for the winter months. Russian butterflies are very large but not as bright as their tropical counterparts. Their coloring blends with the vegetation of Russia's middle belt, its fields, meadows, flowers, and grasses.

FLORA

In Russia forests cover vast areas of land, particularly in Siberia, where they sometimes stretch for hundreds or thousands of miles. The trees in Russian forests are of both the coniferous and deciduous varieties. The coniferous trees include firs, pines, larches, and cedars—all of which are majestic and beautiful with needle-like leaves and a wonderful resinous smell. Russians bring fir trees into their homes and decorate them with glistening ornaments and lights at Christmas time. The deciduous trees growing in Russia include the aspen, oak, maple, poplar, and ash.

The birch tree is particularly loved by Russians. Its slender branches, smooth white bark, and small bright-green leaves that quiver in the wind have always inspired artists and poets to compare it to a graceful young girl.

The brown bear is Russia's national animal and adorns many city and family coats of arms. The distant forefathers of the Russians and other Slavic nations deified this powerful and beautiful animal, often calling it the Master of Forests. They worshipped the animal and offered sacrifices to it; if they did hunt bears, it was only for the purpose of testing themselves against the bear's strength and courage.

In the ancient past, as people hunted, they never said the word for "bear" out loud because they believed that animals could understand human speech and would be forewarned. Instead, people used various descriptive phrases. One of these phrases probably accounts for the word "bear" in Russian: medved *(mid-VYED), which literally means "one who knows where the honey is."*

The double-headed eagle is the state symbol of Russia and was first pictured in the fifteenth century. Initially the insignia of the last dynasty of the Byzantine Empire, the

emblem was brought to Russia when Sophia Palaiologina, a Byszantine princess, married the Great Duke of Moscow, Ivan III. For four centuries, the two-headed eagle remained an emblem for Russia until the 1917 Revolution. It was reinstated as the state symbol by President Boris Yeltsin in 1993.

Through the ages, many meanings have been attributed to the symbol. The most common explanation is that the two heads represent the two parts of Russia—the part in Europe and the part in Asia—and both are equally important.

In pagan times, people paid homage to the birch, decorating it with bright ribbons, flowers, and gifts. The birch was also held in high esteem for other reasons: it made good fuel; its bark could be used for weaving *lapti* (LAP-ti), which are very light and comfortable bark shoes, and also for making special baskets for berries and mushrooms. In ancient times, before paper was invented, Russians wrote letters, notes, and documents on birch bark.

CITIES: MOSCOW AND ST. PETERSBURG

Moscow and St. Petersburg are perceived by many Russians as Russia's twin capitals; for many centuries the cities have competed with each other to hold the dominant position as Russia's chief city.

MOSCOW   The officially recognized capital of the Russian Federation, Moscow is one of Russia's oldest cities; it was first mentioned in chronicles dating to 1147. It has played a major role in unifying the Russian lands into a single powerful state. In the fourteenth century, Moscow became the central point around which the feuding Russian principalities began to unify. It was in Moscow that the Kievan Grand Duke had his headquarters, which served as a fortress for him and his troops. The town began to grow around the fortress, called the Kremlin. It is interesting to note that the medieval Kremlin fortress remains the political and administrative center of the city and of all of Russia. This is the seat of Russia's government, and where the president receives foreign guests.

The city has developed around the Kremlin and the adjacent massive Red Square, which is Moscow's main square. With a 2013 population of nearly

This aerial view shows the city center at the heart of Moscow.

twelve million, Moscow is one of the world's largest cities. It is a large industrial center, with major machine-building and instrument-making plants, steel works, and a large number of factories. It is also a major cultural center, with dozens of theaters, cinemas, art galleries, museums, and stadiums.

Modern Moscow consists of many glass and concrete high-rise office buildings and hotels similar to those of any other city in the world. Moscow also has a great number of historical monuments and fine examples of old churches, palaces, and grand houses of differing styles, which give the city enormous character.

This view of St. Petersburg shows Saint Isaac's Square and the monument to Nicholas I.

ST. PETERSBURG This city is a symbol of modern Russia. From 1924 until 1991, it was known as Leningrad, named after the leader of the Soviet revolution, Vladimir Ilyich Lenin (1870—1924). Whereas Moscow is a bustling, picturesque city that developed over the course of centuries, unplanned, with streets clustering together at random, St. Petersburg is a European-style city designed and built according to a specific plan. It is a city of long straight avenues and regularly contoured squares.

In 1703, Czar Peter I ordered a city to be built on a site he had selected. He wanted this new city to be the new capital of Russia, intending it to be an open door to the West and to play an important role in European life. He named the city St. Petersburg in honor of his patron saint. The construction of the city was extremely difficult, and cost a significant loss of life, since it was built on marshlands. Peter employed Europe's and Russia's best architects, and today St. Petersburg is one of the great cities of the world.

St. Petersburg is Russia's second largest industrial and cultural center (after Moscow), and its second, northern capital. Its 2013 population

Yekaterinburg, on the Iset River, is the fourth-largest city in Russia.

numbered 4.9 million. The city has a large number of beautiful historical palaces, squares, and streets. Its magnificent historical sites—the Winter Palace, Dvortsovaya (Palace) Square, the Admiralty, Saint Isaac's Cathedral, and the Russian Museum—have been listed by UNESCO as among the greatest treasures of world culture.

OTHER REGIONS

There are several other cities and towns of historical significance in western Russia. Among them are Novgorod and Pskov, which before the sixteenth century were independent city-states ruled by local nobles, as well as Vladimir, Tver, Yaroslavl, Ryazan, Smolensk, and Kostroma.

Going eastward, there are many other significant towns. For example, the region around the Volga has always been well settled because it provided settlers with fertile land and the river served as a convenient transportation artery for carrying cargo and people to the north. Nizhniy Novgorod, situated on the Volga, became a major trading center whose fairs won fame worldwide. In the seventeenth century, a chain of fortresses was built along the Volga River in order to hold back the intrusions of nomads from the south and east. These fortresses became the towns of Simbirsk (now Ulyanovsk), Samara, Saratov, and Tsarytsin (now Volgograd). When invasions no longer threatened, the fortresses turned into prospering commercial centers.

Kazan, a Tatar city and former capital of the Islamic Kazan Khannate, stands by itself. Though conquered in the sixteenth century, it has preserved its Islamic features and is now the capital of Tatarstan, a national region inside Russia.

Beyond the Volga are vast steppes (grassy plains), followed by the Ural Mountains, which abound in minerals and precious and semiprecious stones, and are a major industrial region of Russia. This region began to develop rapidly at the beginning of the eighteenth century. The cities here include Chelyabinsk, Yekaterinburg, Magnitogorsk, and Perm.

Siberia's chief towns are situated in its southern regions along the giant Trans-Siberian railway: Irkutsk, Omsk, Tomsk, and Novosibirsk. These towns were built by rich industrialists. The houses there are strong, warm, spacious, and functional. These towns have many beautiful palaces and churches, and theaters built in the classical style. Russia's far east has its own capital cities: Khabarovsk, Vladivostok, and Petropavlovsk-Kamchatskiy. For many years Vladivostok was a closed naval base, and for that reason foreigners were not allowed to visit it. Now it is open to everyone and is developing into a center for Russian-Chinese trade.

The train station in Novosibirsk is the starting point of the Trans-Siberian railroad.

INTERNET LINKS

www.historytoday.com/john-etty/russia%E2%80%99s-climate-and-geography
"Russia's Climate and Geography" explores how Russia's geography influenced its history.

www.geocurrents.info/place/russia-ukraine-and-caucasus/siberia/introduction-to-siberia
"Introduction to Siberia" brings this huge northern region's geography into focus.

www.cia.gov/library/publications/the-world-factbook/geos/rs.html
The US Central Intelligence Agency (CIA) offers the lowdown on Russia's geography.

HISTORY

The embalmed corpse of Vladimir Lenin lies on view in a mausoleum in Moscow's Red Square.

2

RUSSIA'S HISTORY AS A NATION SPANS more than a thousand years. Much of it would make for a great series of action adventure movies, involving Vikings, Mongol invasions, medieval battles on frozen lakes, the burning of Moscow— and behind all the color and excitement, a relentless national effort to push Russia's frontiers further and further southward and eastward. The cast of characters would include, among many outrageous players, a czar who killed his only son in a fit of rage, a ruthless czarina who expanded the empire, and a mad monk. All in all, the tales would chronicle the rise of a military superpower.

The Bolshevik Revolution occurred on November 7, 1917, but is called the October Revolution. At the time, Russia was still using the Old Style, or Julian, calendar and according to it, the day was October 25, 1917. Russia has since switched to the New Style, or Gregorian, calendar used by most of the world.

KIEVAN RUS

Russia's story begins around the fifth century with the Slavic people in the Eastern European region of today's Ukraine. According to Byzantine historians at the time, the Slavs were a handsome, tall, and strong people

Baptism of Prince Vladimir is a fresco in St. Vladimir's Cathedral in Kiev. It was painted by the Russian artist Viktor M. Vasnetsov in 1889.

with fair hair; they were brave fighting men of great endurance, and hospitable hosts in peacetime. Their main occupation was farming. They sowed rye, wheat, barley, and millet, and traded, hunted, and fished.

Beating off forays of aggressive Scandinavian Vikings from the north and nomads from the south, the individual principalities gradually formed a large state that was headed by the grand dukes of Kiev. This loose federation of Slavic tribes came to be known as Kievan Rus. Kiev, now the capital of Ukraine, was located on the main trade route connecting the Baltic Sea with the Black Sea and the Byzantine Empire.

Kievan Rus established trade with the cities of Asia and Europe—Prague, Constantinople, and Baghdad. Over time, the Russian social system gradually became feudal. The tribal nobility—the elders, military leaders, fighting men—appropriated the wealth. The princes seized common lands and gave only small plots to the peasants so that they could maintain themselves and their families by working for the landowners. The feudal lords were called boyars.

In 988, Grand Prince Vladimir I joined the Eastern Orthodox Church and made Christianity the official religion of Kievan Rus. The old idols of the heathen gods were thrown into the river. Orthodox priests, who came from Constantinople, christened the Russians in the water of the Dnieper River.

Kievan Rus flourished in the eleventh century during the rule of Grand Duke Yaroslav the Wise (1019—1054). Under him, it became the largest European state—stretching from the Gulf of Finland in the northwest, to the Black Sea coast and the lower Danube in the south, and from the Carpathian Mountains in the west, to the upper Volga in the east. Foreign kings sought to establish friendly relations with Kievan Rus, and marriage was an important tool of diplomacy. Yaroslav married a Swedish princess, and married his daughters to French, Hungarian, and Norwegian kings.

In the thirteenth century, Kievan Rus was invaded by armies from Mongolia, an empire in the heart of Central Asia. Its leader, Genghis Khan, was a clever, talented, and cruel man. His Tatar armies had conquered much of Asia and now turned towards Kievan Rus and Eastern Europe. Battles raged for decades, but by the end of the 1250s, the severe rule of the Tatar Khans was established in Kievan Rus.

THE RISE OF MOSCOW

The Tatar state called "the Golden Horde" was formed with its capital at Sarai on the banks of the Volga River. Tatar destruction of towns throughout Kievan Rus, and the plundering of the country's riches, set Russia's national development back two centuries.

As the years passed, the country gradually began to recover from the destruction. Towns rose from ruins, becoming the first centers of the struggle for liberation. Moscow grew strong. The city became a great crafts and

This painting by Apollinari Vasnetsov (1864-1933) depicts the court of a feudal Russian prince. Apollinari was the brother of the painter Viktor Vasnetsov (painter of image on opposite page).

trading center in an advantageous position: it was at the crossing of trade routes and far from the outlying districts that were constantly threatened by enemy attacks. In time, Moscow felt it could resist the orders of Khan Mamay, the Horde's ruler, and Mamay sent in an army to set them straight. In 1380, Russians led by Grand Duke Dmitri Ivanovich met Mamay's army at Kulikovo Field near the Don River. The Russians won the fierce battle.

A hundred years later, during the rule of Ivan III (1462—1505), known as Russia's unifier, the Tatars' power came to an end. In 1480 Ivan stopped paying taxes to the Tatars and established Russia's national independence. Under Ivan III's son, Vasily III (1505—1533), all the princedoms and lands of Russia, without exception, were finally unified—some voluntarily, others by force. They formed a new state, bringing to an end the wasteful feudal wars. The economy and culture began to develop rapidly.

IVAN THE TERRIBLE

Under the son of Vasily III, Ivan IV (1533—1584), the state's power continued to grow stronger and changes occurred within the class of feudal lords. Along with the rich landowners, the boyars, there appeared a social group of small landowners—the gentry. They received land from the boyars in return for military service. This social group was later destined to become Russia's dominant social class.

Ivan IV was the first ruler to be crowned Czar of All the Russias. Although he further expanded and strengthened the Russian state, his reign was one of the bloodiest in its history. He instituted a system of terror—the source of his nickname—against both the boyars and the common people. The result was that Ivan gained absolute power and established a new centralized government structure that formed the foundation for modern Russia. Personally, Ivan was a difficult man, subject to uncontrollable fits of rage. In one such rage, he killed his own son. Historians wonder if the czar suffered from a mental illness. In any event, Ivan became known as Ivan the Terrible.

Following his death, there was a period known as the Time of Troubles, when anarchy and instability ruled, one czar often quickly replacing another. In 1613, the *zemsky sobor* (state council) assembled and elected as the new czar Mikhail Romanov, the first ruler of the Romanov Dynasty that would continue to rule Russia for the next three hundred years.

During this time, towns flourished and trade expanded. Caviar, salt, and salted fish were shipped from Astrakhan to other towns; cloth and flax came from Novgorod, Yaroslavl, and Kostroma; leather came from Kazan; and furs from Siberia. Moscow and Nizhniy Novgorod were the largest trade centers. Russia grew even larger—pushing into Siberia and the Far East.

The feudal system continued to grow stronger. The feudal lands were divided into those of the lords and those of the peasants, or serfs. The peasant was allotted land; he worked his own plot as well as the landowner's, but he had to work the landowner's ground first, unpaid. He was, in effect, the landowner's slave. Under these terrible conditions peasant riots often broke out.

Ivan the Terrible sits by the bed of his son, who he murdered in this 1860 painting by Nikolay Shustov.

PETER THE GREAT

In 1689, the seventeen-year-old Czar Peter (1672—1725) inherited a huge country lagging considerably behind Europe. Russia had little industry, no modern army or navy, or any convenient seaports. The system of government was old, sluggish, and awkward. Russia needed outlets to the sea to help its trade and communications with Europe.

In order to defend Russia against Europe's growing military might, Russia also needed a modern army and navy. At that time, a port on the Barents Sea was Russia's only naval outlet. But it was ice-bound for six months of the year, as well as being too far from the center of Russia. The Baltic Sea coasts belonged to Sweden and the Black Sea coasts to Turkey.

Peter introduced many reforms in Russia. He built metalworks so that Russia could produce its own arms (by 1725, there were more than a

Peter I heroically stops marauding soldiers in Narva.

hundred factories in Russia); he also started a textile industry. Trade was concentrated in St. Petersburg, and he built a system of canals connecting the Neva and Volga rivers to make it easier to transport goods from the south to the north.

Peter divided the country into provinces headed by governors. Each governor was responsible for tax collection, the armed forces, and public order. The governors increased the number of officials and formed more complex bureaucratic machinery of government in order to consolidate and maintain the power of the gentry. The estates of the gentry were declared their hereditary property, strengthening the bonds of serfdom. This caused riots and occasional outbreaks of violence in the country.

Peter also reformed Russian education. He ordered new textbooks on mathematics, navigation, physics, and chemistry to be printed in Russian and distributed to schools. He also opened an Academy of Science. All of Peter's reforms helped Russia overcome its industrial and cultural backwardness. As a result, Russia achieved a steep rise in the industrial, scientific, and technical spheres, and became a full-fledged European power.

Meanwhile, during this time, the countries of the Baltic region became involved in a war against Sweden—the Great Northern War (1700—1721)—and Russia became involved as well. The war went on for more than two decades, and in the end, Swedish territories on the eastern coast of the Baltic Sea were ceded to Russia. Finally Russia had maritime access to Europe.

CATHERINE THE GREAT

The Russian Empire made great advances during the reign of Catherine II (1729—1796), who has often been referred to as an "enlightened despot." The highly educated empress introduced limited freedom of speech, and a liberal press appeared. However, a cruel form of serfdom flourished behind the façade of the empress' liberal ideas about the common welfare.

A peasant rebellion (1773—1775) led by Emelyan Pugachev swept through Russia during Catherine's reign. It was the greatest popular revolt in Europe, involving the entire Volga region, and it shook the empire to its foundation. Detachments of rebels conquered a series of towns—Kazan, Samara, Ufa, and Chelyabinsk—and burned down hundreds of landowners' estates. The army finally suppressed the uprising only with great difficulty.

FOREIGN AFFAIRS As a result of Russian alliances in Europe and of the divisions of Poland (1772, 1793, and 1795), Russia received much of the Ukrainian and Belorussian lands and a large part of Poland. Following two bloody wars with the Ottoman Empire (1768—1774 and 1787—1791), the problem of gaining an outlet to the Black Sea was successfully solved, and the Crimean Peninsula and the Sea of Azov became Russian territory. During this time, Russia supported the American fight for independence from Great Britain and established diplomatic relations with the new United States.

Catherine the Great is portrayed in this painting from 1763 by the Russian painter Fyodor Rokotov.

THE PATRIOTIC WAR OF 1812

At the beginning of the nineteenth century, a French army led by the emperor Napoleon Bonaparte invaded Russia. Napoleon made no secret of the fact that he wanted to overrun Russia, to subdue and break the country, and distribute its territory among Turkey, Iran, and Poland.

One summer night in 1812, a French army of approximately six hundred thousand in three columns crossed the Neman River into Russia near Kovno (now Kaunas in Lithuania) without a declaration of war. Napoleon hoped to overwhelm the Russian army with one decisive blow, occupy Moscow, and dictate his terms. But instead, he found himself involved in a protracted war. On September 7, 1812, on the fields near the village of Borodino,

70 miles (112.7 km) west of Moscow, half a million men fought each other in an exceptionally bloody battle. Neither side won decisively, but the Russians retreated and the French captured Moscow. The Russians regrouped, however, while Russian partisans (guerrillas) harassed French supply lines. The French army began to dwindle and retreated from Moscow. They suffered terribly from Russian attacks and the cruel winter. Of the one hundred thousand men in Napoleon's retreating army, only nine thousand managed to return to France.

THE NINETEENTH CENTURY

The defeat of the French brought about a change in Russian national consciousness. The peasants, who had defended their country, returned to a life of slavish servitude under the landowners. Alexander I introduced a reactionary policy of merciless serfdom, military drill, and severe censorship. Military service, coupled with agricultural service, was required for life; peasant children began to receive military training at the age of seven and

A rendering of the Decembrists' revolt in St. Petersburg in 1825

at eighteen were turned into soldiers. Understandably, these harsh policies caused much resentment.

THE DECEMBRISTS' REVOLT   Consisting chiefly of patriotic young officers and intellectuals, a group of revolutionaries dreamed of liberating the country from autocracy. They wanted Russia to become a constitutional monarchy. Because of the month in which they staged their protest, they became known as the Decembrists.

Following the death of Alexander I and the appointment of Nicholas I as the new czar, the conspiring officers led several garrisons to Senate Square in St. Petersburg on the morning of December 14, 1825; they called for freedom and change. The common people did not understand what they wanted and did not support them. On the czar's orders, they were fired upon and, by nightfall, they retreated.

Altogether 579 people were brought to trial and more than a hundred were sentenced to prison and exile in Siberia. Five leaders were hanged. Though they proved unsuccessful, these young conspirators' actions went on to inspire future generations of revolutionaries and reformers.

After the suppression of the Decembrists' revolt, Nicholas I's regime was established and lasted for more than thirty years. He was a rough, cruel man who ruled with the precision and intolerance of a military dictator. Even the slightest criticism of the government was punished. Educational establishments were under vigilant supervision, and strict censorship was introduced in literature. Peasant disturbances were mercilessly suppressed.

Also, after many years of war, the northern Caucasus region became Russian—with the Chechens, Dagestanis, and other Caucasian peoples losing their independence—and Russia grew even larger.

ABOLITION OF SERFDOM   In the 1850s, Russia fought a short, unsuccessful war in the Balkans against Turkey. Losing the war increased opposition to the czar among the progressive gentry. Peasant disturbances also increased. Czar Alexander II (1818—1881), the son of Nicholas I (who had died in 1855), said: "It is better to abolish serfdom from above than to wait for a time when it will begin to abolish itself from below."

Two landlords negotiate the sale of a female serf in this painting (1866) by Nikolai Vasilyevich Nevrev.

Serfdom was abolished in 1861. The peasants gained their personal freedom—a landowner no longer had the right to buy or sell them. A peasant could get married without the permission of the landowner, could conclude contracts and bargains on his own, and could engage in his choice of handicrafts and commerce. The peasants became free citizens with full rights. However, some things did not change; peasants continued to pay a poll tax, and were subject to corporal punishment and military service. In addition, a peasant could leave his village only after paying off all his debts to the landowner, and although the peasants were freed together with the land, the best lands remained in the hands of the landowners.

Reforms were also made at the local government level with the creation of the *zemstvos* (ZYEMST-vo)—a committee responsible for the development of the economy and infrastructure in their region. The law was made more accessible to the majority of people, and schools were opened for the common people.

With these reforms, Russia gradually transformed from a feudal agrarian society to an emerging capitalist industrial power. Food processing, textiles, and machine-producing industries began to flourish. Railroad construction expanded on a massive scale from 1860 to 1890. By the end of the nineteenth century, the Trans-Siberian railroad connecting western Russia with the Far East had been completed.

However, peasant rebellions continued. Secret revolutionary societies formed, and it was one of these—*Narodnaya Volya* ("People's Freedom")—that in March 1881 assassinated Czar Alexander II. Alexander III (1845–1894), the new czar, established a regime of brutal repression. The leaders of Narodnaya Volya were put to death, but workers' disturbances continued, and the first workers' unions were established.

In the 1890s, Vladimir Ilyich Lenin began his revolutionary activities in Russia, and in 1903 founded the Communist Party, the party that would later rule Russia for more than seventy years. In 1894 a new czar, Nicholas II (1868–1917), came to the throne. Little did he know that he would be Russia's last czar.

A REVOLUTIONARY CENTURY

In Russia, the twentieth century began with the unsuccessful war against Japan (1904–1905) for domination in Manchuria, northern China. The Japanese dealt Russia a number of defeats on land and at sea that demonstrated the backwardness of the Russian army, as well as the appalling corruption in the military and state systems.

Czar Nicholas II was said to be a nice man who loved his family, but he was considered a weak and uninformed leader.

It was dissatisfaction with this war that ignited the events of January 9, 1905. On that day, soldiers fired upon a peaceful demonstration of workers who were marching to the Winter Palace in St. Petersburg with a petition outlining the people's needs. More than one thousand workers were killed and five thousand wounded. This brutal action provoked a storm of public indignation. On the same evening, the city was covered with a network of barricades erected by the incensed population. Workers disarmed policemen and organized strikes in many cities, the peasants revolted in the countryside, and military units mutinied. The peak of the revolution came in December—involving armed revolts in several cities. The largest uprising was in Moscow.

In 1918, Russian people stand in a long line waiting to buy milk. In the foreground, a girl sells apples from a basket.

For almost two weeks, government forces were unable to suppress the uprising. The government managed to destroy resistance only after using heavy artillery. Many reprisals followed—unions were banned, newspapers and magazines were liquidated, and many revolutionaries and workers were executed.

However, Czar Nicholas II agreed to some concessions. He allowed the creation of a State Duma, a legislative assembly with very limited powers. Under great pressure, he later granted increased civil rights, including the right to form political parties. Though some factions were satisfied with the czar's concessions, more radical groups saw it as an opening toward far larger goals.

WORLD WAR I

In the summer of 1914, World War I (WWI) broke out in Europe. Russia, along with Britain and France, was drawn into a vast and protracted war against Germany and Austria-Hungary. By 1917 Russia was on the brink of exhaustion, having suffered enormous numbers of casualties in the fighting. Industries collapsed, a food shortage caused widespread starvation, and the Russian people lost confidence and trust in the monarchy. At the front lines, the morale of Russian troops bottomed out.

In the czarist court, Nicholas II was seen as a weak and ineffective leader who was out of touch with the realities of the time. The wealth and excesses of the royal family's lifestyle stood in stark contrast to the dire conditions that most Russians were living—and dying—in, and the public was incensed. Meanwhile, the czarina Alexandra fell under the spell of Grigory Rasputin (1872—1916), a self-styled holy man who critics called "the mad monk."

In 1916, while WWI was raging, Nicholas decided to go to the front lines and take command of the troops there. He played the role of the great

THE MAD MONK

Grigory Rasputin (1869–1916) was an illiterate Russian peasant who was a religious mystic and wanderer. In 1907, Rasputin was invited to treat Prince Alexei, then just three years old. Alexei had been born with hemophilia, a genetic disease in which the blood lacks clotting ability; even a small scratch could potentially lead to a fatal loss of blood. Rasputin's presence seemed to calm Alexei, and the czarina included the monk quite intimately in the family's life from then on.

Government officials who were close to the family did not approve of this strange, mysterious peasant. As Russia teetered on the brink of war and revolution, rumors swirled that Rasputin had brought an evil curse upon the royal family, and therefore upon the nation. Whether his gifts were supernatural or more mundane, there was no doubt that he had gained tremendous personal and political power.

A group of nobles took matters into their own hands. In December 1916, they murdered Rasputin, but the story of his death only fueled more fear and speculation. First the killers tried to poison him with cynanide-laced food and wine, but the poison had no effect. Next they shot him at close range and left him for dead—but he wasn't dead and later tried to flee. Again the assailants shot him and beat him, but still he would not die. Finally they bound the monk and threw him in a river.

Modern historians question the validity of the gruesome tale, thinking it may be exaggerated. Nevertheless, Rasputin's frozen corpse, with three bullet holes in it, was discovered in the river. As it turned out, eliminating Rasputin did not save the czar, as the noblemen intended. Within months, the entire monarchy would collapse and the royal family would be assassinated.

After the Romanovs were murdered in 1918, their remains went missing for many decades. In 1979, some scientists located the long-decayed skeletons in the woods outside Yekaterinburg. Missing, however, were the remains of two of the czar's children. Since 1918, rumors had spread that the youngest daughter, Anastasia, had escaped the massacre. Over time, at least ten women claimed to be the lost princess. However, in 2007, the two missing bodies were found, proving that the entire family died in 1918.

commander, leading his troops into battle astride his steed, but in truth, the czar had little idea how to direct a battle, and his mission was an embarrassing failure.

While he was away, Czarina Alexandra, who was already disliked by both the aristocracy and the public, tried to run the government, and many suspected she was involving Rasputin in the affairs of the nation.

END OF THE MONARCHY

The year 1917 was one of astounding change in Russia. It began with an unprecedented wave of strikes and demonstrations in St. Petersburg, and many clashes with the police. When the army was brought in to quell the uprisings, the soldiers defected to join the demonstrators. The revolutionaries renamed the city Petrograd (it would later be changed yet again to Leningrad), and set up the Soviet (or "Council") of Workers' and Soldiers' Deputies. The Duma, vying for power, established a provisional government with representatives of all political parties.

No longer able to control the events taking place around him, Nicholas II abdicated the throne on March 15. A little more than a year later, in Yekaterinburg in the Ural Mountains, Nicholas, his wife, and his children were all executed by their captors.

THE BOLSHEVIKS SEIZE POWER

The provisional government quickly lost the confidence of the people, since it had proved incapable of ending food shortages or the unpopular war with Germany. On November 7, the revolution entered a second phase. Revolutionaries called Bolsheviks, under the direction of party leader Vladimir Lenin, stormed the Winter Palace in St. Petersburg and arrested the members of the provisional government. There were several reasons for their easy victory. The Communist Party numbered more than two hundred thousand members at that time, was well-organized and disciplined, and was represented everywhere—even in the army and navy. For many years, the party had spread its ideas among all sections of the population, and advanced simple slogans that were comprehensible to the masses, such as "Land—To Those Who Till It," and "He Who Does Not Work Shall Not Eat."

During the first months after the revolution, the new power nationalized land, banks, transportation, and large-scale industry, and established a state monopoly on foreign trade. Russia ceded the Baltic regions, part of Ukraine, and Belarus to Germany in return for getting out of World War I. Lenin became the leader of the first Marxist state in the world.

CIVIL WAR Almost immediately, the country fell into a bloody civil war (1918—1922), during which the Communists (Reds) and monarchists (Whites) fought for control of Russia. The situation was further complicated by the intervention of foreign powers—Britain, France, Germany, Japan, and the United States—who wanted to restore the old order and supported the Whites. It was the Reds who were ultimately victorious, however. Their promise to redistribute the land to the peasants generated a lot of grassroots support. Leon Trotsky (1879—1940), commander-in-chief, restored discipline and fighting efficiency to the army via draconian methods. The Red Army was able to defeat the White generals and their supporters and allies. In 1922 the last foreign troops left Russia and the Communists—under the leadership of Lenin and Trotsky—were able to celebrate their victory.

THE UNION OF SOVIET SOCIALIST REPUBLICS

The former empire broke into several independent socialist republics. After the civil war, the necessity for economic and political cooperation became evident. In 1922, representatives of four republics—Russia, Ukraine, Belorussia (now called Belarus), and Transcaucasia (now Georgia, Armenia, and Azerbaijan)—signed a declaration forming the Union of Soviet Socialist Republics (USSR). During the 1930s, Kazakhstan, Uzbekistan, Turkmenistan, Kyrgyzstan, and Tajikistan joined the USSR; the Baltic states (Estonia, Latvia, and Lithuania) were annexed by the USSR in 1940 at the beginning of World War II (WWII).

In January 1924, Lenin, the founder of the Soviet state and leader of the Russian Communist Party, died. A power struggle followed, and

VLADIMIR LENIN: THE MAN WHO CHANGED RUSSIA

Vladimir Lenin was born in the Volga River town of Simbirsk on April 22, 1870. His family was well off and well educated. Vladimir excelled at school and went to study at St. Petersburg University and later law at Kazan University. In St. Petersburg, he was exposed to radical ideas, including the revolutionary theories of Karl Marx, the founder of modern communism.

He turned into a confirmed leftist after his elder brother, who had supported the overthrow of the czar, was executed in 1887. Lenin joined a revolutionary group, was arrested and exiled to Siberia for three years. After his return, he left Russia and went to Western Europe where he continued to work for radical change.

In 1917, with the help of the Germans, who were at war with Russia, Lenin returned home. He watched the overthrow of Czar Nicholas II and the formation of a new democratic government. Lenin then led the Bolsheviks—the name of the revolutionaries— in what is now known as the October Revolution against the government. By 1919 the Bolsheviks and Lenin were in total control of Russia. In 1922, Lenin formed the Soviet Union, the world's first communist country. He was hailed as a hero by revolutionaries the world over and gave hope to many that—finally—a new age of equality was at hand in Russia.

Achieving that idea, however, required harsh methods and Lenin was not opposed to using them. Under his leadership, the Bolsheviks carried out a campaign of mass killings, torture, and political repression called "The Red Terror" during the civil war that followed the revolution.

Even though Lenin's vision of world revolution was never achieved, and the Soviet Union no longer exists, millions still admire Lenin. After suffering a stroke in 1922, Lenin died on January 24, 1924. Today, his corpse is embalmed and lies on view in a mausoleum in Moscow's Red Square. Hundreds of thousands of Russians and others visit it each year.

Joseph Stalin (1879—1953) eventually won the leadership as general secretary of the Communist Party. He imposed a ruthless dictatorship for the next thirty years.

Stalin's reign of terror in Russia reached its height in 1937. Books and films were heavily censored. Any opposition to the regime was regarded as a state crime, with punishment being death or imprisonment in one of the many labor camps. Purge followed purge, ostensibly in search of counter-revolutionaries and spies—but in fact the fear and suspicion they generated was Stalin's way of increasing his hold on power.

In order to implement Lenin's blueprint for modernizing Russia, Stalin created modern branches of industry and eliminated small farms by merging them into large government-owned collective farms. According to many, this forced collectivization resulted in a widespread famine in 1931 in which more than ten million people in Ukraine starved to death. All land was now owned by the state. With no individual responsibility, agricultural output kept declining, and the largest country in the world found it could not feed itself and had to buy its grain abroad.

The Soviet government, however, made major improvements in education and in healthcare. From 1920 to 1940, almost fifty million men and women became literate. In 1930, universal primary education was introduced. Russia was also the first major country in the world to introduce free health care.

In 1925, the Russian city of Volgograd was renamed Stalingrad in honor of Soviet leader Joseph Stalin. In 1961, Nikita Khrushchev changed the name back to Volgograd to try to undo the former dictator's cult of personality. Even today, however, some residents are nostalgic for the name Stalingrad and want it reinstated.

WORLD WAR II

Soviet Russia feared invasion when Adolf Hitler (1889—1945) rose to power in Germany in 1933. One of Hitler's aims was to destroy Communism. Stalin had tried to avoid confrontation with Germany by signing a secret nonaggression pact with Hitler in 1939. Hitler wanted the pact to ensure that Russia wouldn't attack while he was conquering Europe. Later, he ignored the pact when it suited his plans. On June 22, 1941, Nazi Germany attacked the USSR. Six months later, German troops occupied half of the western part of the Soviet Union. They laid siege to Leningrad and were stopped just short of the gates of Moscow, but managed to reach the Volga River in the south.

A portion of the Iron Curtain barbed wire fencing outside Bratislava, in the former Czechoslavakia

Britain and the United States provided financial and military aid to the Soviet Union. In 1943, following the five-month Battle of Stalingrad, there was a breakthrough. The Germans were eventually driven from Soviet lands in 1944, and Soviet troops entered Berlin on May 1, 1945. More than twenty million Soviet soldiers and civilians died in the war.

PERIOD OF RECONSTRUCTION

In the post-war period, Stalin, suspicious of his Western military allies, consolidated his wartime gains in Eastern Europe and ensured Communist dominance there. He built an "Iron Curtain" of barbed wire and observation towers to separate Eastern Europe from the West. A nuclear arms race with the United States ensued.

After Stalin died in 1953, the new general secretary of the Communist Party, Nikita Khrushchev (1894—1971) loosened restrictions. Thousands of people who had been jailed under Stalin were set free and the country made some outstanding achievements—launching the first artificial satellite and then the first man into space. Housing was improved and thousands of families were given apartments. However, Khrushchev's experiments in agriculture led to a further weakening of the economy. In 1964, as a result of internal politics, Khrushchev was removed from power. A period of stagnation followed.

THE DECLINE AND FALL OF THE SUPERPOWER

Leonid Brezhnev (1906—1982) became the new Soviet general secretary in 1964. His tenure was a period of superficial prosperity, but underlying decay. As time passed, the USSR came to be seen as a country ruled by a

The Cold War is the name given to the relationship between the United States and the Soviet Union that began in 1947 soon after the end of World War II (1939–1945), and ended in 1990. It was essentially a "war" without physical hostilities. At issue were the two nations' opposing political and economic systems: democracy and capitalism versus communism. Inherent in the conflict was the question of worldwide influence and dominance.

The conflict began first in Europe, which was divided between US allies in Western Europe and Soviet allies in Eastern Europe. It then spread quickly around the world as the US and the USSR vied for influence in Africa, Asia, and South America. Both nations formed world-wide alliances aimed at containing the other nation.

The Cold War spawned a nuclear arms race between the two adversaries, with missiles aimed at each other's heartlands. Fortunately for the world, the Cold War remained cold, and a "hot" war between the two nations never took place.

group of old men out of touch with the outside world. Brezhnev approved a Soviet intervention in Afghanistan's civil war, thinking a quick victory there would boost Soviet influence in Central Asia. Instead, the war turned into a debacle for the Soviet Union, and further weakened its failing economy.

In 1985, the new general secretary Mikhail S. Gorbachev (b. 1931) instituted widespread reforms to try to save the Party and the country. He brought an end to the war in Afghanistan, set many political prisoners free, and tried to fix the economy and democratize the government. Yet the old guard Communists, afraid of losing their power, hated him. In August 1991, they tried to remove Gorbachev and reinstate the old Communist system. The coup was defeated by reform-minded Russians led by Boris Yeltsin (b. 1931), who was later elected as the country's new leader.

The unsuccessful coup of 1991 and the emergence of Yeltsin as a powerful political figure marked a turn in events. The USSR, a powerful, unified state for so long, disintegrated in December 1991. It split into fifteen independent countries: the Russian Federation, Lithuania, Latvia,

Mikhail S. Gorbachev

In addition to the potential global annihilation posed by the US–USSR nuclear arms race, the Cold War also spawned the "Space Race." In this undeclared contest, both the United States and the Soviet Union competed for supremacy in spaceflight capability. Success in spaceflight was symbolically seen as proof of ideological superiority.

In this battle of achievement, which took place roughly from 1955 to 1972, the world actually benefited from the intense scientific focus that the two superpowers put into reaching the goal of space flight. The Soviets beat the US to several firsts, such as the launch of Sputnik I in 1957—the first artificial satellite to be put into orbit around Earth—as well as putting the first man,

Yuri Gagarin (above), into space in 1961.

In response, US president John F. Kennedy publicly vowed in 1961 that the United States would have a human land on the moon and return safely to Earth before the end of the decade. Though Kennedy did not live to see it, the promised moon landing took place on July 20, 1969, a monumental space race victory for the United States.

In time, both countries joined together in cooperative space projects, resulting in the building of the International Space Station, which was launched in 1998.

Estonia, Belarus, Ukraine, Moldova, Kazakhstan, Turkmenistan, Uzbekistan, Kyrgyzstan, Tajikistan, Georgia, Azerbaijan, and Armenia.

Today, nine republics cooperate as the Commonwealth of Independent States (CIS): Armenia, Azerbaijan, Belarus, Kazakhstan, Kyrgyzstan, Moldova, Russia, Tajikistan, and Uzbekistan. Founding members Ukraine and Turkmenistan are still withholding ratification, and Georgia withdrew in 2009. The Baltic republics—Latvia, Lithuania, and Estonia—chose not to join the CIS and remain totally independent of Russia.

PUTIN TAKES CHARGE

Yeltsin was reelected in July 1996 but soon suffered a heart attack. This affected his health but he remained in office until 1999. On December 31, he stepped down and named Vladimir Putin (b. 1952) as his successor.

Russian President Vladimir Putin in 2015

By 2000, when Putin began his first term as president, he pledged to change things on two fronts. His foreign policy, he said, was to regain Russia's place in world affairs. His domestic policy was to restore stability, to end what he called "revolutions" that had brought Russia low. These two core objectives have inspired everything that Putin has done since.

In 2008, Putin sent troops into neighboring Georgia (also once a part of the Soviet Union) in response to a conflict over two small regions with strong ties to Russia. The international community was outraged, but did little.

In 2014, the Crimea Peninsula, a part of Ukraine, became the focus of the worst East-West crisis since the Cold War. After Ukraine's president was driven from power, pro-Russian forces seized Crimea. They then voted in an election, which Ukraine declared illegal, to make Crimea part of Russia. In eastern Ukraine, pro-Russian rebels supported by Russia, have been fighting the Ukrainian army to establish an independent territory.

FROM SPY TO STRONGMAN

Vladimir Putin dominates Russia and is a major figure in today's world. He was born in 1952 in the Soviet city of Leningrad (now St. Petersburg) and studied law at the city's university. Soon after graduating, he joined the KGB, the Soviet security police and served as a spy in East Germany. Putin entered the Russian government in 1997, and climbed rapidly to the top. He was elected president in 2000 and reelected in 2004, but was prohibited by law from running for a third term in 2008. He remained in control, however, as prime minister. In March 2011, Putin was elected to a new presidential term.

In the popular imagination of Russia, Putin is admired as a strongman who will revive Russia's historical glory. In December 2014 there was a well-attended art show in Moscow seriously comparing Putin to the ancient Greek strongman Hercules. Putin himself cultivates a macho image by riding horses shirtless, posing with tigers, and displaying his judo skills.

Hate him or love him, the steely-eyed Putin now casts an increasingly long shadow on the world. In 2014, for the second year in a row, Forbes magazine named him the world's most powerful person.

In response to Putin's annexation of the Crimea and his actions in eastern Ukraine, the United States and Europe warned him in 2014 against aggression aimed at Russia's neighbors, demanding that he order Russian forces to leave both areas, and to stop supplying pro-Russian rebels with arms. The Russian president, however, did not budge. Both the European Union and the United States imposed economic sanctions on Russia aimed at hurting the Russian economy. A cease-fire agreement in eastern Ukraine went into effect on February 15, 2015, the result of negotiations between European leaders, Ukrainian leaders, and pro-Russian rebels, but it remained to be seen if the cease-fire would hold. Regardless, the new chill between Russia and the West has led some to warn that it could escalate into a new Cold War.

INTERNET LINKS

www.biography.com/people/ivan-the-terrible-9350679
This biography of Ivan the Terrible includes a video of a Biography Channel TV show about the first czar.

www.historytoday.com/michael-lynch/emancipation-russian-serfs-1861-charter-freedom-or-act-betrayal
This tells the story of the abolition of serfdom in Russia.

www.history.com/topics/russian-revolution
The History site has articles, videos, images, and speeches about the Russian Revolution.

www.historylearningsite.co.uk/russia.htm
This is an article about the German-Soviet War during World War II.

www.smithsonianmag.com/people-places/resurrecting-the-czar-64545030
"Resurrecting the Czar" is a *Smithsonian* article about the discovery of the Romanov remains.

"I cannot forecast to you the action of Russia. It is a riddle wrapped in a mystery inside an enigma ..."
—Winston Churchill (1874–1965), then First Lord of the Admiralty of Great Britain, in a BBC radio broadcast on October 1, 1939. Churchill would go on to become the British prime minister during World War II.

GOVERNMENT

The Kremlin in Moscow is the center of the government as well as a UNESCO World Heritage site.

3

THE RUSSIAN FEDERATION CALLS its political structure a "federal presidential republic." That means the executive power is split between the president and the prime minister, but the president—currently Vladimir Putin—is the dominant figure. The law-making power is represented by the Federal Assembly of Russia. It has two chambers: the State Duma, or lower house (similar to the US House of Representatives) and the Federation Council, or upper house (similar to the US Senate). The judicial power is vested in courts and administered by the ministry of justice.

THE PRESIDENT

The Russian president is elected by popular vote every six years and is limited to a maximum of two terms, or twelve years in office. Originally, the presidential term was four years, but it was amended in 2008 to six years. The president's working office is in the Moscow Kremlin. The president appoints the prime minister to serve as head of government

Regardless of his title, Vladimir Putin is the man in charge of Russia. He was prime minister of Russia from 1999 to 2000, and president from 2000 to 2008. Then, because the constitution barred Putin from a third consecutive term, Dmitry Medvedev became president—and immediately named Putin as prime minister. In 2012, Putin was again elected president.

and ranking official of the Council of Ministers cabinet, which oversees government operations. The president determines basic government and foreign policy, is commander-in-chief of Russia's armed forces, and can veto laws passed by the legislature.

THE FEDERATION COUNCIL

The Federation Council is the upper house of the Russian parliament. Unlike the State Duma, the Council isn't elected directly by popular vote. It consists of representatives of Russia's federal entities. Each entity has two council members. One is elected by the entity's legislature; the other is nominated by the head of the entity's government. The terms of the representatives aren't fixed nationally, but depend on the terms of the entities that chose them. The Council works with the Duma to produce draft laws. The Federation Council also has special powers of its own, including the declaration of a presidential election, impeachment of the president, and decisions on the use of armed forces outside Russian territory.

The State Duma building in Moscow

THE STATE DUMA

The State Duma, or lower house of Russia's parliament, is composed of 450 deputies elected for terms of five years following the 2008 constitutional changes. Any Russian citizen over the age of twenty-one is eligible to run. All bills, even those proposed by the Federation Council, must first be considered by the State Duma. Once a majority of the Duma passes a bill, the Duma sends a draft law back to the Federation Council. If the Council rejects it, the two chambers may form a commission to work out a compromise.

THE JUDICIARY

Three types of courts make up Russia's judiciary: 1) the courts of general jurisdiction, which are subject to the Supreme Court; 2) the arbitration court system under the High Court of Arbitration; and 3) the Constitutional Court. The municipal courts are the lowest courts. They serve each city or rural district and hears 90 percent of all civil and criminal cases. The next level is the regional court system. At the highest level is the Russian Supreme Court. The Constitutional Court is empowered to rule on whether or not laws or presidential decrees are constitutional. If it finds a law is unconstitutional, the law becomes unenforceable and government agencies are barred from implementing it.

The Federal Agency of Security of the Russian Federation- successor to the KGB- is housed in this building on Lubyanskaya Square in Moscow.

LAW ENFORCEMENT

Under Soviet rule, the Committee on State Security (KGB) was the main security agency. It was the world's largest espionage, intelligence, and national security organization, involved in all aspects of life of everyday people in the Soviet Union. The KGB was a secretive and secluded organization, and it operated both legally and illegally. As a result, many human-rights violations occurred. Today the KGB has been replaced with two national security agencies. The Federal Security Service (previously known as the Federal Counterintelligence Service) enforces laws that affect internal security, and the Foreign Intelligence Service enforces laws that affect external security.

LOCAL GOVERNMENT

Local governments are divided into a number of "entities": forty-nine *oblasts* (territories named after large cities), twenty-one self-governing republics that represent each dominant ethnic group, ten autonomous *okrugs* or districts, six *krays* (smaller territories that represent the ethnic minorities), one autonomous oblast, and two cities, Moscow and St. Petersburg, which have federal status.

MAJOR POLITICAL PARTIES

Members of the United Russia Party march on Victory Day in the city of Tyumen.

At the time of the collapse of the Soviet Union in 1991 there was only one political party in Russia—the Communist Party. By 2013 there were forty-eight registered political parties in the Russian Federation. The parties represent all kinds of political and religious beliefs, but there are only four official "parties of power" represented in the Duma.

The main party is United Russia, the party of Vladimir Putin. United Russia is a conservative party that strongly supports Russian nationalism and state power. It controls the Duma with 238 members. The next strongest party of power is the Communist Party of the Russian Federation. It supports nationalism and a return to a communist Russia. It has ninety-two members in the Duma. The third party of power is "A Just Russia," a party that supports democratic reform and more freedom for Russians. It has sixty-four representatives in the Duma. The Liberal Democratic Party of Russia, a very right-wing Russian nationalist party, has fifty-six members in the Duma. Forty-four other parties aren't represented in the Duma but have varying influence in Russia's provincial legislatures.

FOREIGN RELATIONS

Since the breakup of the USSR, Russia's political relationship with its fourteen former republics has not always been positive. There have been many concerns regarding weapons, border security, and ethnic conflict. Military action by Russia in Georgia and Ukraine, both former parts of the USSR, has increased the tensions—especially between Russia and the Baltic nations of Estonia, Latvia, and Lithuania.

In his first years in power, Putin had good relations with the United States and Europe. Germany and Eastern Europe, in particular, are major trading partners with Russia and Russia supplies those countries with natural gas.

In 2003, Putin became the first Russian leader to visit Great Britain since 1874. At first, the United States and Russia moved toward friendlier relations and greater trade when, in 2009, US Secretary of State Hillary Clinton and Russian Foreign Secretary Sergei Lavrov, pressed a "reset" button to clear away years of hostility.

The "reset" didn't work. Since Russia's invasion and annexation of the Crimea, US-Russia relations have entered a deep freeze. The US and Europe strongly objected to Russian aggression against Ukraine and have imposed sanctions on Russia's economy. Unless relations improve, some fear that a new Cold War is on the horizon.

Russian Foreign Minister Sergei Lavrov laughs with former US Secretary of State Hillary Clinton after she gives him a "reset button" in 2009.

INTERNET LINKS

government.ru/en
This is the site of the Russian government in English.

www.russianembassy.org/page/government-of-the-russian-federation
The Embassy of the Russian Federation in Washington, DC has info about Russia and its government.

countrystudies.us/russia/69.htm
Find a more detailed description of Russia's government structure.

worldnews.about.com/od/russia/tp/Political-Parties-In-Russia.htm
Russia's main political parties are explained in detail.

www.theguardian.com/world/2014/apr/17/putin-russia-relations-obama-us-ukraine
This article gives insight into the current state of US-Russia relations.

ECONOMY

People under the lighted signs of the Foreign Exchange create a bustling scene in Moscow.

4

A FTER THE COLLAPSE OF THE Soviet Union in 1989, Russia had to reinvent its economy according to new principles. The Communist system had been based primarily on two ideas formulated by Karl Marx: public ownership of factories, mines, industry, and agriculture; and a centrally planned economy. The Communists believed that since the means of production belonged to the state (and therefore, collectively, to everyone), the state should control everything, including planning, financing, and salaries. Under this system, people were supposed to be content and to work peacefully for the benefit of society.

Over the long term, for many reasons, that style of economy failed. Beginning under Boris Yeltsin, Russia developed an economy that combines capitalist principles—private ownership of the means of production and a free market economy—with some government intervention, in terms of state ownership and regulation. Such a system is called a mixed economy.

The computer game Tetris was designed and programmed by Russian Alexey Pajitnov and released in 1984 when he was working for the computing center at the Soviet Academy of Sciences. He didn't start earning royalties from it until 1996 when he moved to the United States and formed The Tetris Company.

ECONOMIC REFORM

Yeltsin wanted radical economic reforms that would help create a fluid democratic economy. In 1992 he ended price controls on most purchased goods, lifted restrictions on private trade, and began to transfer state-owned enterprises into private ownership.

The Russian people immediately felt the effects of these drastic changes. Prices on most goods increased drastically, while industrial production and national income plummeted. By 1993 more than one-third of Russian citizens were classified as living below the poverty line. Many wealthy citizens moved abroad.

Despite many challenges, by the mid-1990s more than a million new private businesses had been established, employing more than two-thirds of the labor force. Most money-making opportunities from business ownership or employment were available only in large cities such as Moscow and St. Petersburg.

By 2001 the economy began to show healthy signs of steady recovery from the inflation of the 1990s. Three-fourths of formerly state-owned enterprises were now privately owned, and a middle-class population was growing. This led to a boom in consumer purchases of goods and services that had previously only been available to the wealthy. By the end of 2014, Russia had a booming economy. But it was based on Russia's vast natural wealth, especially in oil. When the worldwide price of oil began to decline, Russia's economy suffered and was further hurt by the economic sanctions imposed for political reasons by the United States and Europe.

THE TWENTY-FIRST CENTURY

AGRICULTURE Prior to the Soviet regime's collapse there were about fifteen thousand state-controlled farms, which were run like factories using an inadequate production process. Farmland was divided into collectives of about thirty thousand acres each and further divided into plots.

Homeless people huddle near Red Square in Moscow in 1990.

A family was assigned to work each plot on the collective, and the government purchased the produce at a set price.

Even with the government's attempt to privatize farms, this changed very little. By 1993 about 90 percent of farmland was still controlled by former state farms or collectives, which had been restructured as cooperatives or joint stock companies. The main problem was that people who worked the land for a living could not afford to buy it. Also, agricultural output and grain production in Russia had traditionally been low due to the short growing season, inconsistent climate, and poor quality soil.

In 2002 a new law granted the right for citizens to own, buy, sell, and transfer private agricultural land. By 2012, private ownership of farmland in Russia had jumped to over 50 percent.

Huge combines harvest grain on a collective farm in Bashkiria, Russia.

MILITARY DEFENSE Russia's military defense industry includes weapons manufacturing and aircraft building. Russia is the world's second largest exporter of conventional arms, after the United States—including battle tanks, helicopters, armored personnel carriers, fighter jets, air defense systems, and infantry fighting vehicles. Some 2.5 to 3 million people work in the defense industry, which accounts for about 20 percent of manufacturing jobs in Russia.

AEROSPACE INDUSTRY Aircraft production in Russia is an important industry and focuses mostly on military aircraft. After the dissolution of the Soviet Union, the civilian aircraft industry was particularly hard hit. Many of its planes failed to receive international safety and environmental certifications. By 2005, the situation began to improve as an industry-wide reorganization program was put into effect to improve efficiency. One positive result was a new airplane, the Sukhoi Superjet 100, which first flew in 2008. Other new aircraft are also in the works, and increased production is helping to boost Russia's civil aircraft industry.

SPACE INDUSTRY As part of the Soviet Union, Russia was a pioneer in space exploration. After the fall of the Soviet Union, economic hard times forced the Russian government to radically cut back on its space program. By 2005—2006, however, the boom in Russia's economy brought the program back to life. Under a ten-year budget program (2005—2015), Russian space scientists are planning a number of space projects. These include a new moon orbiter and spacecraft to conduct close-up investigations of the planets Venus and Mars. In addition, the Russians are constructing a number of powerful new rockets, including the R-7, which is capable of launching 7.5 tons (6.8 metric tons) into low Earth orbit (LEO) and the Proton rocket, which will be able to lift 20 tons (18 metric tons) into LEO.

NATURAL RESOURCES Russia possesses incalculable natural resources including oil, coal, gas, metal ores, precious stones, gold, silver, platinum, vast forests, and hydroelectric power.

Most mining and refining of natural resources takes place in the Ural Mountains and along the Volga River. While high quantities of these resources are available, there is much more in the eastern part of the country that remains untapped. This is mainly due to the harsh weather and the rugged, sometimes uninhabited, land.

The country's largest sources of economic income are from gas, oil, metals, and timber, which account for more than 80 percent of its exports. Its petroleum industry is one of the world's largest, and Russia is the largest exporter of natural gas and oil.

INDUSTRIAL MANUFACTURING Russia's manufacturing industry is currently in need of modernization in order to become more efficient and provide a wider range of economic support. Production machinery is outdated and many buildings housing the equipment are old and dilapidated.

The manufacturing industry includes chemicals, farming equipment, electric power generators, durable goods, textiles, foodstuff, and handicrafts. These goods are mostly produced in large cities like St. Petersburg and Moscow. People who seek more job opportunities and higher income must often relocate to these cities from rural areas of the country.

SERVICE INDUSTRY Since Russia opened its borders to outsiders, several new service industries have developed that contribute to the economy. In 2013, about 63 percent of the labor force was engaged in the service industry.

Tourism in Russia is booming. Travel agencies in St. Petersburg and Moscow offer organized tours, from hiking and rafting adventures to train excursions and historical city tours.

Russians are also wired for communication. In 2014 there were six national TV stations and roughly 3,300 local TV stations and more than 2,400 public and commercial radio stations. Russia is also highly "wired," boasting the most Internet service providers in Europe.

THE WORKFORCE Despite the population decrease, Russia has enough labor power to drive its economy. In 2013 it was estimated that the labor force was 75.3 million. Unemployment today is only 5.8 percent, but underemployment is still a big problem.

Russia has faced many challenges and setbacks, but the country's economy shows signs of healthy improvement. The gross domestic product (GDP) in 2013 was $2.553 trillion, and until recently, high oil prices had allowed Russia to increase its foreign reserves.

INTERNET LINKS

www.wsj.com/articles/russia-gdp-to-shrink-3-in-2015-economy-minister-says-1422715453
The Wall Street Journal reports on the state of the Russian economy.

www.aei.org/publication/the-political-economy-of-russian-oil-and-gas
This article explains the importance of oil to Russia's economy.

www.themoscowtimes.com/business/article/russian-space-program-gets-52bln-boost/500157.htmlward_space_program.html
The Moscow Times reports "Russian Space Program Gets $52Bln Boost."

ENVIRONMENT

Rush hour traffic in Moscow adds to the air pollution problems in the city.

LIKE ANY COUNTRY, RUSSIA HAS ITS share of environmental challenges. Many of these problems stem from its Communist history. The Soviets built up heavy industry and weapons development with little or no regard for their inherent danger to air, water, and soil. As a result, industrial pollution has been Russia's greatest environmental problem, and the situation is ongoing, long after the Soviet Union dissolved. Other serious issues include deforestation, inefficient energy use, wildlife protection, and nuclear waste.

MINING

Russia is one of the richest sources of natural minerals in the world. The minerals required in industrial production are in high demand both in Russia and abroad. Mining and exporting gold, platinum, copper, iron, nickel, coal, and precious stones are lucrative economic activities for Russia. Unfortunately, this desperately needed source of income also takes a heavy environmental toll on the land.

5

Russia is known as "the lungs of Europe" because it has vast forests that soak up carbon dioxide emissions from Europe's industrial regions to the west. The Russian forests are second only to the Amazon rainforest in the amount of carbon dioxide they absorb.

A poisoned and oil-covered bird lies dying in front of local volunteers removing oil pollution from the Black Sea shore in the port of Kavkaz in November 2007.

Mining has been profitable for the country, but the result has been nearly catastrophic. As far back as the eighteenth century, minerals have been extracted from the Ural Mountains. Mining may take years to completely deplete an area of its minerals, but once the resources are gone, they cannot be replenished. Also, heavy extraction of the earth's natural resources destabilizes the land, and alternative forms of use are difficult to identify.

OIL DRILLING

Oil spills cause major environmental problems because they are difficult to clean up. At this time no method has been developed that does a completely efficient job. Once a body of water is contaminated with oil, it can destroy aquatic life and make the water uninhabitable for many years.

In 2014 Russia was the world's largest supplier of crude oil. The oil and natural gas industries are vital to the Russian economy, but exploration, production, and spills have taken a toll on the land.

AIR POLLUTION

An environmental report issued by the Russian government indicated that air pollution in most major cities exceeds safe levels, and drinking water is also at risk. These risks contribute to health problems such as chronic respiratory disorders, heart disease, and high cancer rates. More than 30 percent of Russian children are born with pollution-linked diseases or physical defects. Emissions from road traffic, heavy industry, and coal-fired power plants contribute to unhealthy levels of toxins in the air.

Over the past several decades many Russian citizens have moved from small towns to large cities such as Moscow and St. Petersburg to find work. Since more vehicles are required for inner-city transportation, pollution in large cities is greater than in small towns.

Other major contributors to air pollution are Russia's iron and steel manufacturing plants, some of which have been in operation for more than sixty years. Several cities were established with the sole purpose of supporting iron and steel production. The cities of Perm, Chelyabinsk, and Magnitogorsk are examples, and they continue to be the locations for major industrial manufacturers today.

The city of Perm dates back to 1723, when it was established for copper smelting. The city provided easy access to the Volga River and was part of

Smoke from incinerators billows over St. Petersburg.

an important transportation route. Today it remains a heavily industrialized city with approximately eighty factories that represent the aircraft, electrical, chemical, oil, timber, and engineering industries.

In 1929 the city of Chelyabinsk was established on the bank of the Ural River for the purpose of mining the area's iron ore. In the mid-1970s the plants here produced 15 million tons of ore per year. That eventually led to the depletion of the iron ore deposits.

WATER POLLUTION

Most freshwater sources in Russia are polluted. The Russian Environment Ministry estimates freshwater resource damage will cost an estimated $2.3 billion to correct. Most of the water is contaminated from sewage and manufacturing runoff. Some threatened freshwater sources are the Kola and Selenga Rivers, and Lake Baikal.

Wastewater from a pulp and paper plant pours through a reservoir in Baikalsk, Siberia.

The Kola River is located in the Kola Peninsula of the Arctic region that borders the Barents and the White Seas. The Kola Peninsula covers 40,000 square miles (100,000 sq km) and is the world's largest supplier of phosphorus. The contaminants released there affect the freshwater and marine ecosystems. The Kola River is one of several rivers that release pollutants into the Arctic Ocean.

The Selenga River is located in east-central Russia and is the main source of water for Lake Baikal. Domestic waste from large cities and industrial waste from chemical plants and pulp and paper mills contribute to its pollution.

Lake Baikal is located in southern Siberia. It is a clear blue, banana-shaped body of freshwater surrounded by a vast landscape of plants and trees, many of which are more than five hundred years old. The lush greenery provides a natural habitat for many bird and animal species. More than 2,500 species of aquatic life and more than a thousand species of plants in the lake have been documented; some are endemic and others are also found in other parts of the world.

Some two-thirds of Lake Baikal's shoreline is protected as a nature reserve, but research shows that the lake is polluted by chemical residue from manufacturing runoff. One source of pollutants is the waste dumped from a pulp and paper plant located on Lake Baikal's southern shore in the city of Baikalsk. It was built in the mid-1950s and, because of a combination of poor law enforcement and lack of environmental regulation, chemical residue from the plant has been released into the lake for many years.

The nerpa seal is a species unique to Baikal, the world's deepest lake.

More than five hundred rivers, brooks, and streams throughout Russia flow into Lake Baikal bringing runoff from industrial plants, mining sites, and farms. It will take years to restore Lake Baikal to a semblence of its natural state.

ENDANGERED WILDLIFE

Only eighteen species of seal exist today. While most live in oceans, a few, like the nerpa seal, inhabit freshwater lakes such as Lake Baikal.

The nerpa seal is the smallest of its species. It measures between 47 and 55 inches (1.2 and 1.4 m) long and weighs between 138.9 and 154.3 pounds (63 and 70 kilograms). It has a life span of fifty-two to fifty-six years.

The nerpa seal population has declined due to pollutants in its natural habitat. The seals have suffered from reproductive problems, food contamination, and lower natural immunity. In addition to these

An eagle owl soars low over a long grassy meadow.

problems much of their shoreline habitat has been lost to land development. The nerpa seal is also hunted for its fur, fat, and meat.

The Eurasian eagle owl is the largest owl in the world. It measures between 23 and 29 inches (58 and 73 centimeters) in length, has a wing span of 60 to 79 inches (150 to 200 cm), and weighs between 3.5 and 9.3 pounds (1.6 and 4.2 kg).

Mostly brown in color with a white speckled coat, the eagle owl makes its home in the northwestern and central regions of Russia, as well as in Siberia. It subsists mostly on a diet of small rodents like mice, squirrels, and hedgehogs, but is capable of killing young deer and other animals of comparable size.

The eagle owl is in danger of extinction because of deforestation, which limits its hunting and nesting areas. Another threat to this giant bird-of-prey is polluted food sources. When toxins get stored in the fat cells of the small rodents on which the bird feeds, it can reduce the reproduction rate as well as the life span of the eagle owl.

ENVIRONMENTAL PROTECTION

In 1993 the Center for Russian Environmental Policy (CREP) was founded, the first of several actions to indicate that the Russian government has become more environmentally sensitive. The goal of the CREP is to educate the public and encourage ecofriendly legislation. A year later, the terms of the Agreement on Cooperation in the Field of Environemntal Protections, originally laid out in 1972, were renegotiated and updated. Then, in 2004, Russia ratified the Kyoto Protocol, an international accord that requires countries to help reduce air pollution. More than a hundred countries have already ratified the agreement.

The former Soviet government acknowledged the importance of taking care of the environment. It had set aside more than 160 nature reserves in many biosphere-dependent areas and provided generous funding for scientists to study and support the continuation of various plant and animal species. Unfortunately, this awareness and funding was not extended to the manufacturing and mining industries. After three quarters of a century of generating industrial waste it will take many decades to repair the damage done to the Russian environment. The current government is discussing steps to prevent further damage. At present, success depends on the modernization of manufacturing plants and proper industrial residue disposal.

A bike pavilion near the entrance to the sprawling Muzeon Art Park makes bikes available to rent for visitors.

INTERNET LINKS

www2.epa.gov/international-cooperation/epa-collaboration-russia
The US Environmental Protection Agency discusses partnerships with, and projects in, Russia.

rbth.com/science_and_tech/2014/09/05/russias_battle_with_water_pollution_continues_39577.html
Water pollution in Russia continues, according to a Greenpeace report.

www.rferl.org/media/photogallery/russia-endangered-species/24915307.html
Radio Free Europe offers a slide show of Russia's endangered species.

RUSSIANS

An indigenous Nenet child is bundled up in fur in Nadym,
a town in the far north of central Russia.

6

THE UNITED STATES OFTEN celebrates the diversity of its people, but it's not the only country with a multiethnic makeup. Russia, too, is a land of many peoples, but unlike in America, Russia's racial, religious, and ethnic diversity did not come primarily from immigration. Rather, over the centuries, the country expanded over vast distances, absorbing different populations along the way.

The Russian people are made up of nearly two hundred nationalities and ethnic groups.

This trend began in the fourteenth century, with the founding of the Moscow-centered Russian state. Over the next few centuries, because of the rapid outward expansion in Russia, the people of Siberia, the Volga region, the Far East, and the northern Caucasus became a part of the Russian state, with Moscow as their distant focal point. Sometimes expansion was achieved peacefully, but sometimes it came about by more forceful means.

THE EMPIRE

In the nineteenth century, Russia became a colonial power, but unlike England, France, Holland, and Spain, Russia's colonial expansion was not overseas, but involved swallowing up surrounding territories on the European-Asian landmass. Among these territories were the northern part of the Caucasus, Turkestan (including present-day Uzbekistan),

Kyrgyzstan, Tajikistan, and Turkmenistan. Some highly developed, complex European cultures, such as Poland and Finland, were also added to the Russian Empire as a result of military conquest.

People from all corners of the empire traveled to the Russian center in order to study and trade. Sometimes they stayed there, diversifying and enriching Russian life and culture. The Ukrainians, another Slavic people, make up the largest ethnic minority after the Russians and Tatars. Another Slavic people, the Belarusians, make up only a small percentage of the population in the Russian Federation. The process of migration occurred in both directions: many ethnic Russians now live in former Soviet republics such as Ukraine, Belarus, Latvia, Lithuania, and Kazakhstan.

From ancient times, various peoples such as Armenians, Georgians, Kazakhs, Uzbeks, and Azerbaijanis have lived in Russia. Russia also has populations of Jews and nomadic Roma (Gypsies). For hundreds of years, many rulers and governments tried to make the Roma live in permanent settlements, but to no avail. With the creation of an independent Jewish homeland, and the history of Russian violence toward Jews, many of Russia's Jews have emigrated to Israel.

THE SOVIET CITIZEN

In Soviet Russia, the official policy was to create a new type of citizen who no longer identified with a region or republic, but with the ideology of the party—a "universal" citizen, dedicated to international socialism. International marriages and migration to other republics within the Soviet Union were encouraged.

Nowadays, it is evident that this experiment failed. After the breakup of the USSR, national differences quickly surfaced. Nationalism rapidly increased, both in Russia and in the former Soviet republics. The many years of suppression of national identities under the Soviet regime led to an explosion of nationalist feeling in all parts of the former USSR. Sporadic local wars flared up in many of the distant outposts of the former Soviet Union, particularly in the northern Caucasus, Armenia, Azerbaijan, Moldavia, and Chechnya.

ETHNIC DIVERSITY

According to 2014 statistics, the population of the Russian Federation is about 142 million, of which about 78 percent are Russians. These Russians are not a single homogeneous group but originate from a variety of ethnic backgrounds. For example, Russians living in the north—in Murmansk and Arkhangelsk—or in Siberia, or in the areas bordering Ukraine, are significantly different from each other in their customs and attitudes. Russia's enormous size makes such variations inevitable between people thousands of miles apart.

A Siberian husky dog pulls a boy on a tube across the ice in Buryatia, Russia.

The modern Russians bearing the closest resemblance to their Slavic ancestors are probably those who live just north of Moscow—the inhabitants of Pskov, Arkhangelsk, and Novgorod. They are fair-haired and blue-eyed, with lean, narrow faces. Asian features are not common in this part of Russia.

SIBERIANS The inhabitants of Siberia represent another type of Russian. Settlers originally came to Siberia in the seventeenth century to escape the religious reforms under Peter I. They were adherents of the "old faith" and refused to recognize church reforms and modernization; nor would they accept outsiders into their community. They settled in isolated areas, and have managed, to some extent, to maintain to this day the customs, habits, and dress style of traditional Russians.

In the nineteenth century, many more people from Ukraine, Belarus, and western Russia migrated to Siberia to escape poverty and to gain new land.

Under both the czars and communism, Siberia has been used as a place to which political prisoners were sent, and many of Siberia's inhabitants are the descendants of those people.

Members of a Chechen family

COSSACKS Cossacks originate from the northern hinterlands of the Black and Caspian seas. The term was applied to peasants who fled from serfdom in Poland, Lithuania, and Muscovy to the Dnieper and Don regions, where they established free, self-governing, military communities. The Russians used the Cossacks to expand their empire eastward and eventually annex Siberia. In Russia's 2010 population census, Cossacks were recognized as an ethnicity.

TURKS Another significant national group are the Turks. These people live mainly around the lower Volga. They include various ethnic groups, such as the Tatars, Bashkirs, Mordvinians, and Udmurts. They tend to have round faces, slanting cheekbones, narrow eyes, and a short and stocky figure inherited from their ancestors who were nomadic horsemen.

MOUNTAIN PEOPLES Different peoples and nationalities live in the Russian Caucasus. These are the peoples of Dagestan (consisting of dozens of small groups and tribes), the Chechens, Ossetians, Karachayevans, Circassians, Cabardins, and Balkars. Each group has its own individual history and customs. The Ossetians, for example, are the last people to speak the language of the ancient Scythians.

PEOPLES OF THE POLAR NORTH In the ice-bound northern regions of Russia, there live small groups of indigenous peoples. Among them are the Nenets, Chukchis, Komis, Evenks, Yakuts, and Koryaks. These peoples still maintain their ancient languages, which has made them of great interest to philologists and anthropologists.

Some equally small ethnic groups live in the warm south of Asian Russia and in the Far East—the Buryats, Nakasses, Altays, Tuwins, Nganasanes, Yukaghirs, and Tofalars.

THE CZAR'S SHOCK TROOPS

Of all the peoples who came under Russian rule, the most feared were the Cossacks. They were a warrior people living in the forests and plains north of the Black and Caspian Seas. They were magnificent horsemen and riflemen. At the beginning of the 1500s, there were six "hosts," or armies, of Cossacks: the Don, the Greben, the Yaik, the Volga, the Dniepler and the Zaporozhian.

A painting of Russian Cossacks

The Russians used the Cossacks as defenders of the Russian frontier and also as advance "shock troops" for the territorial expansion of the Russian Empire's borders eastward and southward. The Cossacks were also the first Russian settlers of the vast cold expanses of Siberia. In the nineteenth and twentieth centuries, the tsar used Cossacks to suppress unrest and revolutionary activities. Rumors of an impending Cossack raid often spread terror through Russian villages.

INTERNET LINKS

www.rferl.org/content/new-russian-nationalities-policy-sparks-outcry/24786140.html

"Rumblings In The Republics: New Russian Nationalities Policy Sparks Outcry" examines the friction between the Russian government and various nationalities.

siberiantimes.com/science/casestudy/features/f0055-is-this-the-face-of-an-ancient-amazon-female-warrior

The *Siberian Times* offers an interesting look at the artistic recreation of an ancient female warrior from remains found in southern Siberia

joshuaproject.net/countries/RS

This site lists 180 nationalities and ethnic groups in Russia, their population numbers, and their religions.

LIFESTYLE

A little girl wears a traditional kerchief and a necklace of cracknel, or round biscuits, and carries a samovar.

7

THE LIFESTYLE OF THE URBAN
and rural populations in Russia differ
sharply, as in most other countries
in the world. Moscow and St. Petersburg
are cosmopolitan, and have many of
the same characteristics as cities in
Australia, Germany, and the United States.
Skyscrapers, however, are fewer and lower,
and public transportation, once a source
of pride in the USSR, is suffering from
declining government subsidies.
Road traffic, on the other hand, is
increasing rapidly.

"Russia cannot
be understood
with the mind
alone. No ordinary
yardstick can span
her greatness:
She stands alone,
unique—In Russia,
one can only
believe."
—Fyodor Tyutchev
(1803–1873),
nineteenth-
century
Russian poet

CITY LIFE

The clothes worn by urban folk are of an international style—men usually wear European-style jackets, trousers, shirts, and ties, and women wear dresses or blouses with skirts or slacks. Food has also been internationalized—people living in Moscow can eat Chinese, Korean, Indian, French, Italian, and other cuisines.

The work schedule dominates people's daily routine in the cities. On workdays, household chores are done when time permits, and most

A Russian woman enjoys working in her vegetable garden.

are done over the weekend. The norm in Russia is a five-day workweek with two days off, usually Saturday and Sunday. One of the days off is devoted to household affairs and the other is usually spent on entertainment, walks in a local park, or visits to the cinema, theater, museum, parents, or friends. City dwellers pay little attention to the changing seasons, except perhaps to change their attire. National and religious differences are less noticeable, and everyone spends their work time and holidays side by side, in the same offices and visiting the same restaurants, theaters, and sports stadiums.

The political liberalization in Russia has led to an explosion in the variety of social activities available in the city. New societies, clubs, and associations have sprung up everywhere, whether political, cultural, artistic, or environmental. In place of the former Communist Party publications there have appeared new and independent newspapers and magazines, such as *Daily Kommersant*—the first daily business newspaper in Russia—and *Delovaya Gazeta*. As in most countries, however, technology is becoming the primary vehicle for communication.

SUMMER ACTIVITIES People from the city usually try to go on vacation in summer to enjoy the warmth of the sun and admire Russia's plethora of flowers, forests, and meadows. It is an interesting paradox that until recently thousands of people, especially the young, have been deserting their native villages for the cities, while at the same time millions of city dwellers have been doing the opposite—trying to get closer to the land by joining gardening societies and dacha (DAH-cha—"country chalet") cooperatives. About twenty million urban families spend every weekend from April to October tending their gardens—planting vegetables, fruit, and flowers.

Children who live in the cold northern regions have their own specific amusements and games. They do not fear the long winter, for this is the time to ski, skate, ride dog sleds, fish through holes cut into the thick ice, and race reindeer.

And what fun it is for children, after spending some time skiing in the freezing cold, to come home and sit by the fire, enjoying thin slices of freshly frozen pink fish meat and drinking sweet, strong tea.

COUNTRY LIFE

Life is quite different in the countryside. Even nowadays, when many urban customs have been introduced into village life and many past traditions have been forgotten, some of the centuries-old customs and rites survive and flourish.

Russia's traditional lifestyle is of a rural nature, since for many centuries most Russians were peasants who worked the land. Village life still depends on the cycle of the seasons. Peasants divide the year's work as follows: sowing and harvesting, grazing the cattle, plowing, hay-making, hunting, collecting fruit, stocking up firewood, and spinning.

Schoolchildren listen to a lesson in a small, ungraded country school.

The annual folk calendar, a crystallization of the wisdom of many generations of country folk, previously regulated their entire life, from birth to death. These traditions have helped the people to survive despite natural disasters and life under both czarist and Communist repression, and have given their lives a fixed structure.

EDUCATION

In Russia, education is compulsory and provided by the state. Public school begins at the preschool level, when children are five years old. The children play games and are taught to read, write, and count.

Formal education begins at age six and continues for nine to eleven years, depending on the schools the child attends. Children go to school six days a week, Monday through Saturday. The school year begins in September and ends in May. It is divided into four terms, with vacations of up to two weeks between the terms.

Students make a robot at the World Robotic Olympiad in Sochi, Russia, in 2014. The event was attended by delegates from forty-seven countries.

Russia also has a number of special vocational high schools, where a general education (language, mathematics, physical education, and science) is combined with technical training and some on-the-job experience. In a similar style are the junior colleges (institutes)—places where the students can concentrate on engineering, medical, musical, or art courses, as well as receive a general education. Higher education begins at around age eighteen and lasts for five or six years. Again, all higher education is state funded, although students have to attain the appropriate grades to be allowed to continue.

In the nineteenth century the general emphasis had been on learning for learning's sake. Under Soviet rule, emphasis was on preparing students to perform "socially useful labor." There was a heavy stress on engineering and the sciences needed for industry, and courses in Marxism-Leninism were a mandatory part of the curriculum. Moscow University was perceived as the Harvard of the Soviet Union. Today, a new fact of life is that rich Russians prefer to send their children to private schools and universities abroad,

something that was not possible in Soviet times. Moreover, entrance into new private grammar and high schools is sought after, much for the same reasons as in the United States. There is a perception that they provide a better, well-rounded education; they also serve as a status symbol for the family.

It has been said that during the period 1965—1985, serious harm was inflicted on the Russian education system and that young people were prevented from demonstrating the true extent of their abilities by perfunctory instruction and the drive for uniformity.

Current reforms being applied to the system are aimed at making it a more democratic institution, where students play a more active role in their own education and do not study just for the sake of obtaining good grades.

A bride and groom pose in front of St. Basil's Cathedral in Moscow.

BIRTH, MARRIAGE, AND DEATH

Traditional rituals connected with birth, coming-of-age, marriage, and death, are still of an essentially religious nature, despite seventy years of Communism. These rituals, although they differ greatly from religion to religion, are observed for the same reasons. Christians baptize their newborns, while Muslims and Jews circumcise their male infants. These two rites have a similar significance in that they are performed for spiritual purification. Death rites are also similar—relatives and friends pay their respects and wish eternal peace to the deceased.

Under the Communist system, it was usual to have a local Soviet councillor officiate at weddings, filling the role of priest. The practice of exchanging rings and vows was still followed. With Russia's recent liberalization, more people are opting for a traditional-style wedding conducted by a clergyman of their chosen religion. However, divorce has become a serious problem in Russia. In 2014, Russia had the highest divorce rate in the world—five divorces per thousand people, according to the UN *Demographic Yearbook*.

In the 1920s and 1930s, attempts were made to do away with the old rites and rituals, replacing them with new, "socialist" practices. Easter, Christmas, and New Year festivities were abolished and branded as "remnants of the past." Religious feasts were replaced by celebrations of the birthdays of revolutionary leaders and anniversaries of revolutions in various countries. Today, celebrations connected with revolutionary figures and events are declining in popularity, and old festivals are being restored.

Traditional wedding padlocks hang on the Luzhkov Bridge over the bypass canal in Moscow. The "locks of love" celebrate newly-wedded devotion.

INTERNET LINKS

www.justgorussia.co.uk/en/russian_people.html
This site presents a generalized overview of the lifestyle of the Russian people.

www.themoscowtimes.com/opinion/article/how-self-sacrifice-has-shaped-the-russian-soul/471668.html
The *Moscow Times* offers an essay, "How Self-Sacrifice Has Shaped the Russian Soul."

www.dw.de/russia-an-educational-system-in-crisis/a-15906118
The article "Russia: An educational system in crisis" takes a look at recent reforms and alleges that corruption is undermining the school system.

RELIGION

The Cathedral of Christ the Saviour shines in the sunlight in Moscow.

8

ORTHODOX CHRISTIANITY IS BY far Russia's largest religion. Some 75 percent of the population belong to the Orthodox Church. Islam comes in a distant second, with only 6.5 percent of the population. However, in certain regions, particularly in parts of the Caucasus, Muslims make up the majority religious population.

Moscow's Cathedral of Christ the Saviour was blown up in 1931 by Joseph Stalin during his attempt to drive religion out of Soviet life. After the fall of Communism, it was rebuilt in the 1990s. It is the tallest Orthodox Christian church in the world.

The Kul Sharif Mosque in Kazan is one of the largest mosques in Russia.

Russian Orthodox Patriarch Kirill holds a cross in Moscow's Red Square during a procession celebrating Saints Cyrilius and Methodius' Day.

Small Jewish and Armenian populations and their religions can also be found within the borders of the Russian Federation, as well as Buddhist communities on Russia's southern and eastern borders. Following the Communist authorities' persecution of all religions in Russia for most of this century, many of the churches are currently undergoing a revival in Russia's more liberal climate.

CHRISTIANITY

THE RUSSIAN ORTHODOX CHURCH Christianity, as was noted in previous chapters, came to Russia in the tenth century from Byzantium. Following the East-West schism of 1054, when Christianity was divided into the Orthodox and Catholic religions, Christianity's Eastern branch, the Greek Orthodox Church, prevailed in Russia. The translation of the Greek term

"orthodox" means "doctrines that are held as right or true," and hence the official name of the Church in Russia is the Russian Orthodox Church. In the course of five or six centuries, Christianity was introduced into pagan Russia with difficulty and often by force, but on the whole, the process was peaceful, without any massacres or destruction of towns.

The Russian Orthodox Temple in the city of Irkutsk, Siberia, is an example of Neo-Byzantine style.

Later, the Orthodox Church became so firmly established in the lives of the people that it was felt to be an integral part of most Russians' consciousness. After the fall of Constantinople to the Ottoman Empire in the middle of the fifteenth century, Russia became the chief custodian of the precepts of Orthodoxy and remains so to this day, despite the Communists' attempt to suppress it.

To explain the doctrines of Orthodoxy in full is too great a task for this book. We shall only mention that the code of its basic dogmas, the so-called creed, binds every follower of the Orthodox religion to believe in the triune

RELIGIOUS PERSECUTION

Ever since the reforms of Peter I, the Russian Orthodox Church has been dependent upon the state. The clergy received salaries from the state and were considered mere state officials "concerned with religious affairs."

Soon after the 1917 Revolution, by a decree of the Soviet powers, the Church was separated from the state and made independent. Its first act was the restoration of the Orthodox Patriarchship, which had been banned by Czar Peter. Freedom to profess and practice any religion was allowed, and religious belief was henceforth considered a matter of individual conscience. This progressive step made by the Soviet powers put all religions in Russia on an equal footing.

The new authorities did not maintain their even-handed attitude for long. Atheism became state policy in the 1920s, and this set off a campaign of persecution of the churches and believers. Clergymen of all religions were herded into labor camps and prisons and branded as "parasites of the working people." Churches and temples were closed down, and their decorations—including those that were of a great artistic and cultural value—were either stolen or destroyed. The buildings were blown up or, at best, used as storehouses, workshops, or club houses. It is impossible to say now how many churches, mosques, and synagogues were destroyed during this period. Religious literature was confiscated and destroyed, and reading the Bible was equated with counter-revolutionary activity. People were not allowed to baptize their newborns or to perform funeral rites for their dead.

The poster says, "Ban religious holidays."

This state of affairs lasted until 1942–1943 when, amidst the heavy casualties of World War II, the state decided to use religion to boost patriotism in support of the war effort. Some churches were opened, and people talked about the need to wage a "sacred war" against the non-Orthodox German aggressor. After the war, state opposition to religion was resumed, first under Stalin and then under the more "liberal" Khrushchev. Again, ancient churches were destroyed, icons burned, and believers persecuted. Many churches were turned into museums.

In the 1970s and 1980s, under the pressure of world opinion, the Orthodox Church was allowed to exist, but only if it limited its role to "promoting peace on earth through prayer." In the 1990s, religion was revived in Russia, and the number of followers of different faiths continues to grow. The once confiscated churches, monasteries, and church property have been handed back to the clergy. It has again become a national custom to celebrate religious holidays like Christmas and Easter for Christians, Eid-al-Fitr and Eid-al-Adha for Muslims, Yom Kippur for Jews, and Vesak Day for Buddhists, as well as many other festivals.

God: God the Father, who created the earth; God the Son (Jesus Christ), who came from heaven to be born of the Virgin Mary, be crucified under Pontius Pilate, and on the third day be resurrected from the dead and ascend into heaven; and God the Holy Spirit, who proceeded from God the Father. This is set forth in clauses one to eight of the creed. Clause nine binds the believer to revere the one holy and apostolic church. Clauses eleven and twelve tell the faithful to expect resurrection from death and eternal life after Judgment Day. The Russian Orthodox Church is headed by the Patriarch of All Russia and does not recognize the Pope.

Some nationalities living in the northern Caucasus, including the northernmost people of Ossetia, profess the Orthodox faith, which reached them via Georgia. Many people in this region are Muslims, however. In the Middle Ages, Christian missionaries preached the new religion among the pagans of northern Russia and Siberia and managed to baptize such groups as the Komis, Permyaks, Maris, and Mordvinians.

An Armenian church in the city of Pyatigorsk in the Caucasus

OTHER CHRISTIAN CHURCHES The Orthodox faith differs from Roman Catholicism in a number of religious beliefs and details pertaining to rites and rituals. Nevertheless, it is more similar to Catholicism than to Protestantism. In the Russian Federation, Catholicism has a small number of followers, chiefly among Poles and Lithuanians who have settled there.

The number of Protestant churches is also small. There are, as well, various small groups of Evangelists, Seventh-Day Adventists, and Jehovah's Witnesses, whose popularity is growing.

Armenians have been settling in Russia for many centuries. Large Armenian colonies exist in Moscow, St. Petersburg, Rostov-on-Don, Astrakhan, and other large cities. In each of these places, a branch of the Armenian Church was established. Today, functioning Armenian churches have remained in only a few Russian towns. The Armenian Church is also Christian and considered a branch of the Gregorian Church, which, although similar, differs in some aspects of dogma from both Orthodoxy and Catholicism.

JUDAISM

In the nineteenth century, Jews were terrorized and oppressed in Russia, particularly in the southwestern regions (today's Ukraine and Poland). Waves of anti-Jewish riots swept through Jewish communities from 1881 to 1884, and again from 1903 to 1906, culminating in the World War I and postwar years, 1917—1922. During these anti-Semitic events, bloodthirsty mobs destroyed Jewish property, and raped, injured, and killed thousands of Jews. Some 50,000 to 250,000 lives were lost.

The pogroms drove massive waves of Russian Jews to emigrate from their homeland. For those who remained, Jewish religious practice was suppressed for decades by the Soviet regime, offering little opportunity for generations of Jews to follow the faith. In the 1990s more and more synagogues were opened as people felt free to attend them. Today there is a core Jewish population of 190,000 people in Russia.

ISLAM

The Islamic religion is Russia's second largest religion. It is professed mainly by peoples living in the Volga region—the Tatars and the Bashkirs—and by some peoples of the Northern Caucasus— Chechens, Ingushes, and Dagestanis. They mostly belong to the Sunni branch of Islam. There are no local variations of Islamic teachings, and dogmas, customs, and prayers follow those laid down by the Prophet Mohammed.

The colorful Temple of All Religions in Kazar is a complex of buildings serving sixteen religions.

INTERNET LINKS

countrystudies.us/russia/38.htm
This is a history of the Orthodox Church in Russia.

islam.ru/en/content/story/islam-russia
Islam.ru is an information portal on Islam in Russia.

www.jewishvirtuallibrary.org/jsource/vjw/russia.html
The Jewish Virtual Library has a history of Jews in Russia.

www.pewforum.org/2014/02/10/russians-return-to-religion-but-not-to-church
The Pew Research Center has an in-depth study of religious trends in Russia.

LANGUAGE

The Saints Cyril and Methodius are called the Apostles to the Slavs. They are credited with creating the Glagolitic and Cyrillic alphabets.

9

W ITH NEARLY TWO HUNDRED
different nationalities and ethnic
groups, each with its own language,
Russia is a patchwork quilt of languages.
Ethnic Russians account for about three-
quarters of the Russian Federation's
population, so it is natural that Russian is
the most widely spoken language. Although
all ethnic groups living in Russia use their
own national languages, a knowledge of
Russian is something most of them have—
it is the common language of Russia and
the Commonwealth of Independent States.
For example, a Ukrainian would speak
Russian to a Buryat.

Какйе языкй
вы знáете?

(kahk-EE-ye yah-
zik-EE vi ZNAH-
ye-tye?)

"What languages
do you know?"

HISTORY OF THE RUSSIAN LANGUAGE

Russian belongs to the Eastern branch of the Slavic language family,
which has its origins in Indo-European. In the sixth through eleventh
centuries a common East Slavic root language developed from the
ancient Slavic language common to all Slavs. In subsequent centuries
this East Slavic root language diverged into several languages: Russian,

An old bronze plaque is written in the Cyrillic alphabet.

Ukrainian, and Belorussian. Two other branches of Slavic also developed: West and South Slavic. Languages that belong to South Slavic are spoken in the former Yugoslavia, Macedonia, and Bulgaria; languages of West Slavic are spoken in Poland, Slovakia, and the Czech Republic. Because of Hungary's proximity to these countries, people mistakenly assume that Hungarian is also a Slavic language; it is not. Hungarian belongs to the Finno-Ugric branch of Uralic.

The linguistic scenario outlined above is complicated by other factors. One of the important influences on the development of Russian arrived in the church books that reached Kievan Rus through Bulgaria after the acceptance of Christianity by Prince Vladimir. These books were written in what is known as Old Church Slavonic. As a result, Old Church Slavonic became superimposed on the language spoken in Kievan Rus. As Muscovy grew more powerful and important in the fourteenth to sixteenth centuries, Great Russian, or simply Russian, developed there. During Peter the Great's reign, the Russian language borrowed many words from Western Europe, particularly scientific, technical, navigational, and administrative terminology.

In the eighteenth and nineteenth centuries, the Russian language further developed amid fighting between the supporters of the older language and those of the rising new style that brought the literary, written language closer to the language spoken by the people. A major influence in this debate was Mikhail Lomonosov (1711—1765), who wrote the first scholarly grammar of the Russian language, in which words were classified according to "styles"—high, medium, and low.

Major changes to the language came about at the beginning of the nineteenth century, thanks to the writings of Alexander Pushkin (1799—1837), the father of Russian literature. Pushkin synthesized various levels of language—composed of folk, Old Church Slavic, and words from Western European languages—to create a new literary language. Many consider him the founder of modern Russian and its phonetic, grammatical, and lexical standards. He had as much influence on the development of the Russian language as Shakespeare had on English.

Orthodox clergymen, city authorities, and city residents march along the Kremlin Wall to mark the Day of the Cyrillic Alphabet, May 24, 2010, in Moscow.

Although in the past two centuries the language has changed a lot and the number of borrowed words has increased, Russians still mainly speak the language in which Pushkin wrote his prose and poetry.

THE CYRILLIC ALPHABET

The oldest treasures of written Russian date back to the eleventh century. Earlier examples have not been preserved, or are as yet undiscovered. Experts believe that some kind of written language existed before this time. For example, a tenth-century Arabian traveler mentions that he saw some inscriptions and a name on the tomb of a Russian nobleman. However, it is unknown what kind of inscription this was.

The alphabet of all the Slavic languages that is used today, with some minor differences, by Russians, Ukrainians, Belarusians, Serbs, and Bulgarians, was created in the middle of the ninth century by the brothers Cyril and Methodius. They were two monks involved in translating Byzantine church texts (written in Greek) into the Slavic script. This alphabet consisted

of thirty letters—some borrowed from the Greek alphabet and others specifically invented to convey the sounds of the Slavic languages that did not exist in Greek. Cyril and Methodius were canonized for their great achievement. When Kievan Rus adopted Christianity in the tenth century, it gained not only books from Byzantium written in Greek, but also books from Bulgaria written in the Slavic script—the Cyrillic alphabet of Cyril and Methodius. This alphabet became the basis of the written Russian language. The Cyrillic alphabet was preserved through the course of centuries in both manuscript form and in the first printed books.

Under Czar Peter I, the so-called civilian script, which was simpler and more convenient for printing, was introduced. This is the script used today.

The Cyrillic alphabet has also been used to create written languages for those peoples of the USSR that before the 1917 Revolution did not have a written language: the nations of the far north, the Bashkirs, the Buryats, the Kabardino-Balkars, the peoples of Dagestan, the Komis, the Maris, the Mordvinians, and the Yakuts of northern Siberia.

"The Battle of the Ice on April 5, 1242, at Lake Peipus" is a page from a manscript from around 1568.

NON-SLAVIC LANGUAGES

Apart from Russian, people in Russia also speak languages belonging to other groups, such as Turkic, Finno-Ugric, and Iranian. Much about the history of these languages has intrigued linguists and scholars.

The people living in the Urals and the Volga region—the Bashkirs, Udmurts, and Maris—speak languages that are very closely related to Hungarian and Finnish. Linguists believe that these peoples were once related and that they migrated together with the Hunnic hordes of the conqueror Atilla during the great movement of nations in the fourth and fifth centuries. They traveled

through the expanses of Asia to Europe and partially settled down, reaching the Danube River and Pannonia (an ancient Roman province in central Europe), where they created the Magyar state, now modern Hungary. Some also traveled north and settled in Finland.

A vendor selects a copy of the *Vedomosti* daily newspaper at her street stall in Moscow.

NAMES

Russian names dating back to pagan times have practically died out. Only a few have remained and today sound more like nicknames. Some of them sound almost incomprehensible to modern Russians, for example, Yermak, Zhdan, Kruchina, Metla, Pervoi, Tomilo, Nezhdana, and Shchap.

After the conversion of Kievan Rus to Christianity, people began to be given new, Christian names. During the first centuries after conversion people had two names—an old pagan one, and a new Christian name given in baptism.

There was once a *Svyatsy* (svYA-tzy)—a church calendar in which every

day was marked with the names of saints or Biblical personages. A newborn child would usually be given one of the names falling on the day of his or her birth or close to it. Usually, these were names borrowed from the Old or New Testament. From these origins, certain names became nationally popular. Common male names include Ioann (Ivan), Andrei, Pavel, Pyotr, Filipp, Luka, Matfei (Matvey), and Mikhail; female names include Maria, Anna, Marfa, Elizaveta, and Tamara.

This list was increased by names taken from the Byzantine Greeks—Feodor, Georgy (Yuri), Konstantin, Nikolai, Vasily, Alexander, Alexei, Lev, Lydia, Irina, Sofya, Taisia, and others, as well as purely Russian names like Boris, Gleb, Svyatoslav, Vladimir, and names borrowed from Scandinavia—Askold, Oleg, and Igor.

Patronymics (a name derived from the given name of the father) are traditional in Russia. If the father's name is Ivan Krylov, then the son's name, for example, will be Pyotr (given) Ivanovich (patronymic) Krylov (family). Likewise, the daughter's name will be, for example, Natalia Ivanovna Krylova. Friends often address each other by both the given name and the patronymic; however, both names are always used when addressing one's superiors.

In the post-revolutionary 1920s, it was the fashion to give "revolutionary" names such as Marat, Zhores, Spartak, and Engels. There were also some very strange names reflecting the new social and political realities—Idea, Raketa, Diktatura, Avangard, Elektron, Revoliutsia, and Traktor! There even appeared some strange-sounding names that were abbreviations: Voenmor (the Russian abbreviation for the navy), Melor (Marx, Engels, and Lenin, the founders of the revolution), and even Dazdraperma (the first syllables of the Communist slogan "Long Live May Day"). After Lenin's death, there appeared many names that were adaptations of his name. For example, Vladlen, Lenina, Vilen, or Ninel. All these names have long ceased to be anything but a joke.

Today, the most popular names are derived from Greek and other European languages. One exception is the female name Indira, reflecting the late Indian prime minister Indira Gandhi's popularity in Russia.

The names of the peoples of the far north are quite original. Some are difficult to pronounce and very complicated: Akhakhanavrak, Kutyakhsiuk, Eketamyn, Yarakvagvig, and Ememkut. These names have clear-cut meanings, much like those traditionally used by Native Americans. Some, like Volna and Groza ("wave" and "thunderstorm"), reflect natural phenomena, while others are definitions of human qualities and properties ("he who owns many reindeer" or "one who is not afraid of evil spirits").

INTERNET LINKS

www.omniglot.com/writing/russian.htm
Omniglot offers an introduction to Russian language and the Cyrillic alphabet.

learnrussian.rt.com/alphabet/the-history-of-the-cyrillic-alphabet
This site has a history of the Cyrillic alphabet.

russiapedia.rt.com/prominent-russians/science-and-technology/mikhail-lomonosov
This is a biography of Mikhail Lomonosov.

ARTS

Anna Pavlova, the popular Russian prima ballerina, is pictured around 1905.

10

PHILOSOPHERS SAY ART IS BORN OF suffering. If that is so, then surely Russia has given its artists fertile ground. Whatever their source, the Russian arts are a great contribution to world culture. Over the course of nine centuries, Russians have produced outstanding works of architecture, painting, music, and literature.

The Hermitage in St. Petersburg is one of the world's largest and oldest museums. Its collection of art and artifacts consists of some three million objects from the Stone Age to the present.

The Winter Palace and Hermitage Museum in St. Petersburg was once a residence of the czars.

ARCHITECTURE

In Kievan Rus, churches were the first and best stone structures to be built. In 1037 construction began on Saint Sofia's in Kiev. This was Kievan Rus's first stone cathedral and was built by architects who had come from Byzantium. The cathedral is on the UNESCO World Heritage list.

Gradually, a national type of church developed. It was called a four-pillar church because the vault was supported from the inside by four pillars. A church could have a different number of domes: one (symbol of Jesus Christ), three (symbol of the Trinity), or five (symbol of Jesus Christ and four Apostles). Magnificent eleventh- and twelfth-century cathedrals have been preserved in Vladimir, Novgorod, and Pskov, as well as in Kiev in Ukraine.

Russian architecture revived after the liberation of Kievan Rus from the Mongols and the establishment of the centralized Moscow state at the beginning of the fifteenth century. Century after century, splendid cathedrals and monastery buildings appeared inside the Kremlin fortress to symbolize the might and unity of the Russian state.

ICONS

Inside Orthodox churches, one will find icons. The art of icon painting came to Kievan Rus from Byzantium and achieved a very high standard. The icons brought from

Constantinople were highly revered and considered sacred in Russia. One of them, "Our Lady of Vladimir" (eleventh or twelfth century), which according to legend was said to have been painted by the Apostle Luke, had been miraculously preserved in Vladimir.

An icon is not just an ordinary painting. It is a special type of religious image that the artist imbues with divine energy, so that the image becomes, for believers, an aspect and expression of God. Icon painting methods are meant to evoke an ethereal quality in order to illustrate a religious idea.

Large eyes are a dominating feature in faces depicted on icons, symbolizing the superiority of the spirit over the body. The background is usually gold and is intended to elevate the representatives of God—the saints and martyrs—from everything earthly.

Before starting work on an icon, the artist prays and fasts. This prepares the artist to receive the divine spirit which is understood to be the true source of the artwork.

The palace of Peterhof is a UNESCO World Heritage site.

The remarkable Saint Basil's Cathedral (built 1555—1561) in Moscow's Red Square is unequalled in Russian architecture. It was designed on Ivan the Terrible's orders to honor the capture of Kazan in 1552. It is a cluster of nine colorful tower-like churches, each crowned with a dome, all of which are connected by internal vaulted passages and surrounded by a circular gallery. Saint Basil's is such an iconic building that it is often seen as a symbol of Russia itself.

When the new capital of St. Petersburg was being built in the early 1700s, architects were invited from Holland, Italy, and Germany to build a city that was more European than Russian. Some of the original eighteenth-century buildings from Czar Peter's time have been preserved to this day, including the Saints Peter and Paul Cathedral, Peter I's palace in the Summer Garden, and Menshikov's Palace.

During Catherine II's reign, Bartolomeo Rastrelli (1700—1771), a gifted Florentine architect who came to Russia as a young man, built many palaces and churches in St. Petersburg and other towns. Among his works are the Winter Palace and the palaces of Peterhof and Tsarskoye Selo. By lavishly embellishing the palaces, he created grand buildings

in the Baroque style, dramatically changing the appearance of Peter's St. Petersburg.

Italian architect Carlo Rossi (1775—1849) contributed to the grandeur of St. Petersburg; he designed the Mikhailovsky Palace (now the Russian Museum) and added the final touches to the Dvortsovaya Palace and Senate Squares. In Moscow, he supervised the building of the Main Headquarters and Theatra Inaya Street.

The artist Vasily Vereshchagin dedicated his painting, *The Apotheosis of War* (1871), "to all conquerors, past, present and to come."

PAINTING

In the early 1860s, a group of artists formed an association of painters who worked together and discussed new literature and art. The *peredvizhniki* (pere-DVIZH-neekee), meaning "itinerants" or "wanderers," as member artists became known, depicted peasant life in a realistic style; they also produced many landscapes of the beautiful Russian countryside. Their interest in the often difficult life of the Russian peasants led to a greater awareness on the part of the Russian intelligentsia of the social and moral problems facing Russia.

One of the most famous of them was Vasily Perov (1834—1882). His

ALAMEDA FREE LIBRARY

Natalia Goncharova (1881-1962), seen here in her *Self Portrait, 1907*, was an important Russian avant-garde artist.

paintings present a panorama of Russian life in the second half of the nineteenth century. There was no subject he considered unworthy of his art—be it poor children pulling a barrel of icy water on a sledge, a village funeral, or a rural religious procession with a drunken priest.

Vasily Vereshchagin (1842—1904) painted many battle scenes, exposing the essential inhumanity of war. His most famous canvas, *The Apotheosis of War*, depicts a huge mountain of skulls—the result of one of the campaigns of the ancient conqueror Tamerlane—and bears the inscription: "To all the conquerors of the past, present, and future." The heroes of folk and epic tales can be seen on the canvases of Victor Vasnetsov (1848—1926). The most famous of them, *The Epic Heroes*, depicts legendary warriors who defended Russia against the Mongol invasion.

One of the most famous Russian artists of the twentieth century was Marc Chagall (1887—1985). Forced to leave the Soviet Union due to difficulties with the Communist authorities, he spent much of his time in exile, mainly in France. He was a prolific painter and book illustrator. Many of his works reference Jewish folk tale and religious themes. His most popular works have a fantastical, dreamlike quality, evoking memory and nostalgia.

Kazimir Malevich (1878—1935) was one of the great innovators in art and a pioneer of the Russian avant-garde. He is associated with a movement called Suprematism, which concerned, among other things, the use of color to create the illusion of space. One of his most famous paintings is *Black Square* (1923). His art has been exhibited in galleries around the world.

LITERATURE

The nineteenth century has been called the golden age of Russian art and culture, for it was then that Russia's greatest works were created in literature, painting, and music.

Alexander Pushkin (1799—1837), Russia's most prominent national poet, is seen as the father of modern Russian literature. His many works—*Eugene Onegin* (1833), a verse novel, *The Tales of Belkin* (1830), a cycle of realistic stories (the first in Russia), the historical drama *Boris Godunov* (1825), and hundreds of poems—are considered treasures of Russian literature. He was on friendly terms with the Decembrists and addressed one of his poems to the exiles in Siberia. In an effort to subdue and win over the famous poet, Czar Nicholas I appointed him to court service. Tormented by the nobility and persecuted by creditors, he died defending his honor in a duel with a Frenchman. Crowds of people came to his apartment in St. Petersburg to pay their last respects. Pushkin's work represents in embryonic form almost all the literary genres that developed later in the nineteenth century.

The work of Nikolai Gogol (1809—1852) marks another important stage in the development of Russian literature. In his novel *Dead Souls* (1842) as well as in the play *The Inspector-General* (1836), he satirized the vices specific not only to Russia with its serfdom but to all of mankind—the ignorance, legalized corruption, greed, and self-interest of the bureaucracies that

Music (1920) by Marc Chagall, is one of four panels for the wall of the Moscow Jewish Theater.

"All we can know is that we know nothing. And that's the height of human wisdom."
-Leo Tolstoy, *War and Peace* (1869)

are part of absolutist, autocratic governments. Gogol was also the first to portray in literature the "little man"—the world of urban commoners, petty officials, paupers, and the destitute. Gogol's story "The Overcoat" (1842) is considered a classic in which the everyday and the fantastic, the real and the unreal, the serious and the comical are brought together to capture the quality of human life.

REALISM By the middle of the nineteenth century a more realistic style of writing came into prominence. It was characterized by rich and detailed imagery, attention to psychological description, and a deep interest in conveying the private and public lives of people of various social strata.

The work of Fyodor Dostoyevsky (1821—1881) still continues to have an enormous influence on world literature. Unequalled in his gift for psychological penetration, he understood better than anyone the torment of the "little man," the humiliated, insulted, and oppressed people of czarist Russia. His novels *Crime and Punishment* (1866), *The Brothers Karamazov* (1880), and *Possessed* (1872) are among the great works of world literature.

The second half of the nineteenth century saw the rise of another great writer— Leo Tolstoy (1828—1910). In his novels *War and Peace* (1869), *Anna Karenina* (1877), and *Resurrection* (1899), he vividly reflected life in Russia, with all its complexities and contradictions. Tolstoy was able to bring to life a whole gallery of characters from various social classes. He was a master at capturing the tensions and conflicts that are part of family life.

In his short stories, Anton Chekhov (1860—1904) portrayed the human condition in the cities as well as in the villages. His writing reveals that he was a great observer who was able to depict the lives of all kinds of people— be it in the slums or in the drawing rooms of the day—in a way that was convincing and true to life. Many of his subjects were unhappy in some way; they often lived in a state of melancholy and boredom, as they talked of a better life to come in the future. Chekhov is also famous for his plays. Three of his well-known plays are *Uncle Vanya* (1900), *The Three Sisters* (1901), and *The Cherry Orchard* (1904). They continue to be staged in Russia, Europe, and the United States.

MUSIC AND BALLET

MUSIC In the nineteenth century, Russian musical genius blossomed. Peter Tchaikovsky (1840—1893) is probably Russia's greatest composer. His six symphonies, the operas *Eugene Onegin*, *Queen of Spades*, and *Mazepa* (all based on Pushkin's literary works), and the ballets *Swan Lake*, *The Nutcracker*, and *The Sleeping Beauty*, represent collectively the summit of nineteenth-century Russian music. The composer could convey, with tremendous force, the joy, suffering, and conflicts of humankind. Tchaikovsky's works are still popular the world over. The works of other composers—Modest Mussorgsky, Alexander Borodin, and Nikolai Rimsky-Korsakoff—are also acknowledged masterpieces of nineteenth-century Russian music.

In the twentieth century, the traditions of the previous century were continued by the brilliant composers Alexander Skriabin, who reflected

A New Year's performance of Peter Tchaikovsky's *The Nutcracker* is presented on the stage of the ZIL Cultural Center in Moscow.

the approaching momentous social changes, Sergei Rachmaninoff, who spent much of his life in exile in Europe and the United States, and Igor Stravinsky, who composed the controversial ballet *The Rite of Spring* (1913).

BALLET Russian classical ballet is considered the greatest in the world. There are two main ballet companies in Russia: the Bolshoi in Moscow, and the Kirov in St. Petersburg. Both are world-renowned.

At the beginning of the twentieth century, the impressario Sergei Diaghilev (1872—1929) organized extremely successful tours in Europe for his company, Ballets Russes, starring one of the greatest dancers the world has ever seen, Vaslav Nijinsky (1890—1950). Nijinsky gained legendary status for his extraordinary dramatic virtuosity, strength, and feather-weight movement.

Russia's greatest female dancer was Anna Pavlova (1881—1931). She also toured with Diaghilev's company and achieved international fame for her discipline, grace, and poetic movement. Rudolf Nureyev (1938—1991), who defected to the United States in 1961, was Russia's best-known postwar dancer; a master of fast turns and suspended leaps, he was considered the true heir of Nijinsky.

Mikhail Baryshnikov in New York City in 2013

Like Nureyev, the acclaimed Soviet dancer Mikhail Baryshnikov (b. 1948) defected in 1974 to Canada so he could pursue greater opportunities in the West. He joined the New York City Ballet and then later the American Ballet Theatre, where he became artistic director. Baryshnikov became an American celebrity and had roles on Broadway as well as in films and TV.

THE SOVIET PERIOD

Under Stalin's oppressive regime in the 1930s, 1940s, and 1950s, the creative arts were put to the service of the state. The task of the Soviet writer and artist was to educate the masses in the spirit of Communist Party ideology, foster allegiance to the state, and glorify its ruler, Stalin. Socialist realism, a style formally adopted in 1934, was the only acceptable method; it called for portraying life through rosy lenses, placing emphasis on the "paradise on earth" that the workers were building.

After Stalin's death in 1953, there was a brief period of literary freedom when writers tried to depict the personal lives of their heroes, not just their accomplishments at the workplace. In cinema, *The Cranes are Flying* (1960) and *Ballad of a Soldier* (1960) won world acclaim for their sensitive depiction of the impact of war on private lives. On the other hand, the writer and poet Boris Pasternak found himself more and more persecuted by the authorities. In 1957 he sent his great novel *Dr. Zhivago* to Italy after being unable to publish it in the USSR. Pasternak was awarded the 1958 Nobel Prize in Literature but was "talked out" of attending the ceremonies.

There was another hiatus from government regulation in the early 1960s. The major literary event at the time was the publication of

Soviet dissident Alexander Solzhenitsyn takes notes during his journey through Siberia upon his return to Vladivostock in 1994 after years of exile in the United States.

In 1974, Alexander Solzhenitsyn was deported from the Soviet Union and stripped of his Soviet citizenship. He eventually moved to Cavendish, Vermont, where he lived for almost twenty years. In 1994, after the dissolution of the Soviet Union, Solzhenitsyn and his wife returned to Moscow where he lived until his death in 2008.

Alexander Solzhenitsyn's *One Day in the Life of Ivan Denisovich* (1962). This novel depicted in great realistic detail the physical and spiritual effort it took to survive one day in one of the Stalinist labor camps in the north. This was the first time the topic of labor camps was written about openly, and the work's publication electrified the nation.

A year later, however, at a Moscow art exhibition, Nikita Khrushchev denounced abstract art and literary experimentation in the strongest, crudest terms. For safety's sake, the boldest writers managed to have their manuscripts smuggled abroad and published there, which is how Solzhenitsyn published his *Gulag Archipelago* (1973—1975). It is still considered one of the most important books of the twentieth century.

POST-SOVIET ARTS

With the liquidation of censorship amid the new freedoms in post-Soviet Russia, many new writers emerged. One of the most successful new writers in Russia today is Viktor Pelevin; his stories have been translated into several European languages as well as English. Pelevin's works, such as the collection of stories *The Blue Lantern* (1991) and the novel *Generation P* (1999), revolve around the question of what reality is. They can be engaging and entertaining as well as deeply philosophical. His 2014 release, *The Love for Three Zuckerbrins*, was an instant best-seller in Russia.

Vladimir Sharov's novel, *Return to Egypt*, won the 2014 Russian Booker Prize for Literature. It is imbued with biblical motifs and attempts at rethinking Russian history. Dystopian novels have become very popular in Russia, just as they have in the West. *The Day of the Oprichnik* (2012) by Vladimir Sorokin imagines Russia in 2027, when the country is under the rule of a twisted dictator, and the people are terrorized by the Oprichniki, the medieval secret police created by Ivan the Terrible.

The Russian movie *Leviathan* (2014), directed by Andrei Zvyagintsev, received international acclaim, including a nomination for an Academy Award for Best Foreign Film of 2014. The movie, a story of small town corruption, is seen to be a thinly-disguised criticism of the Putin regime.

INTERNET LINKS

www.theguardian.com/film/2014/nov/06/leviathan-director-andrei-zvyagintsev-russia-oscar-contender-film

In this article from *The Guardian,* the director of the film *Leviathan* discusses life under Putin.

www.darkroastedblend.com/2013/01/totalitarian-architecture-of-soviet.html

"Totalitarian Architecture of the Soviet Union" offers an excellent overview, with many pictures, of the monumental, excessive style of the Communist period.

www.dartmouth.edu/~russ15/russia_PI/Russian_art.html

Dartmouth College's page on nineteenth-century Russian art: "Ideological Realism," offers information and images.

www.rusmuseum.ru/eng/home

The Russian Museum site in English has information about the St. Petersburg museum, its collections, and exhibitions.

www.russianballethistory.com/sergediaghilevfounder.htm

This site offers information on the legacy of Sergei Diaghilev.

www.biography.com/people/aleksandr-solzhenitsyn-9488509

Biography.com offers a brief look at the life of Alexander Solzhenitsyn.

www.marcchagallart.net

Many images of Marc Chagall's works, as well as his biography, can be found here.

LEISURE

A girl with a snowboard admires the view from atop a peak in the Sheregesh Ski Resort in the Kemerovo region of Russia in 2013.

11

EVERYONE NEEDS SOME DOWN TIME, some time for socializing, for hobbies, or just for relaxation, and Russians are no different. They like to visit their friends and play host to guests. When visiting friends, relatives, or parents, it is customary to bring a simple gift such as a homemade pie, a box of candy, a bottle of wine, or perhaps a small toy for the host's children.

Being the largest country in the world, it isn't surprising that Russia boasts the world's largest number of mountain ranges. Russia's most famous ski resorts are in the Caucasus and Ural mountains, but various lesser-known ski resorts are scattered around the country.

Russians enjoy the sandy beach at Kulikovo on the Baltic Sea.

A hiker walks by a mountain lake in the Altai Mountains.

PASTIMES

In summer, Russians like to go swimming in their local river or lake, and go mushroom- and berry-picking in the forests. This is easy for villagers, but not for city folk, who have to make a trip to the countryside by train or car. During the Soviet years, recreational centers were built in the villages, containing enough room for a library and movie theater, as well as space for all kinds of other activities, such as singing, dancing, and painting.

Village people can also visit a theater or museum in the nearest town. In Russia, even the smaller towns have their own local museums—often rather good ones—built, as a rule, before the 1917 revolution by rich patrons of the arts. Often, the rich merchants, after collecting a number of paintings, built a special house for the collection and presented it to their hometown.

The most famous among them was Pavel Tretiakov, a Moscow merchant who owned a large collection of eighteenth- and nineteenth-century Russian art. He presented his art collection to the city of Moscow at the end of the last century. Today, the State Tretiakov Gallery is one of the biggest museums in the world.

On the whole, the type of recreation Russians choose depends upon their personal inclinations—some prefer reading a book, others prefer a game of chess, and still others like to tinker with their car over the weekend.

For the young and athletic Russia there are active pastimes such as country hikes, mountain climbing, and journeys down rivers in canoes and kayaks. The "new Russians," or those who have acquired wealth recently, also like to travel to Europe and the United States. For people living in the north of Russia, the most favorite recreation is traveling to the south and the warm Black Sea coast to get as much sun as they can to last them through the long northern winter.

In recent times television has become extremely popular, especially among children. Viewers in the main urban centers enjoy access to a number of television and radio stations as well as the Internet. Of course, some regions have more channels than others. Moscow, for example, has a number of channels for educational purposes, and both Moscow and St. Petersburg can receive each other's local television signals.

Some outdoor enthusiasts go white water rafting on the Chulishman River.

Television was used as an efficient instrument for testing and analyzing Russia's spirit of openness, known as glasnost (GLAS-nost), in the late 1980s. In the 1990s a number of programs focused on recent political and social upheavals in Russia and the rest of the Commonwealth of Independent States. Some parliamentary sessions were also televised. Under Putin independent television stations have been closed, and the government, once more, is moving toward control of television and radio.

The skating rink at the All-Russia Exhibition Centre in Moscow is the largest ice rink in the world.

PHYSICAL ACTIVITY AND SPORTS

Since ancient times, Russians have practiced various physical exercises, games, and contests, both as a form of education and as preparation of young Russians for times of war and hardship. In the first half of the nineteenth century, sports schools, clubs, and societies began to appear in Moscow, St. Petersburg, and Kiev. Regular sports competitions were held in the country, financed by rich landowners, merchants, and aristocrats. In the late nineteenth century, workers' sports organizations also began to appear in Russia.

In 1896 P. Lesgarf instigated a scientifically based system of physical education called Courses for Physical Training that became the prototype of most sports institutes created in the USSR after the 1917 revolution. Russia was one of twelve countries in 1894 that decided to revive the Olympic Games and set up the International Olympic Committee.

After the 1917 revolution, sports and physical training became an integral part of life in the USSR. In the 1930s, fitness programs were instituted to prepare people for work and defense. The benefit of these programs became evident during World War II, when the Russian people were tested to the limits of their endurance by the hardships of war. In Soviet times, in many industries, people briefly interrupted their working day to exercise. Sports were practiced via a wide range of sports clubs, organizations, and groups. This network belonged to the trade unions and was wholly financed by them.

Under Soviet rule, achievements by the country's sports figures in world competitions were a source of major pride. Such sportsmen were funded by the Soviet government, but managed to retain their "amateur" status for international competitions and the Olympics.

Russia's major sports societies—CSKA (the Central Sports Army Club), Spartak (the trade unions), Lokomotiv (railway workers), and Dinamo (the Interior Ministry)—have major soccer, basketball, and ice hockey teams with millions of fans in Russia. Baseball is popular, and the first national baseball championships were held in 1989.

Today, there are both voluntary and compulsory sports in Russia. Compulsory exercise programs are a part of the school curriculum, from kindergarten to college level, as well as of the army routine. Sports stars and members of national teams are now paid regular salaries rather than a government stipend for their services. They also sign regular contracts. Over the last few years, a number of Russia's top soccer players have moved to Europe to play for teams there, where players' salaries are more generous than in Russia.

Little boys run in a children's competition in the Physical Culture Institute in Moscow.

INTERNET LINKS

www.tristarmedia.com/bestofrussia/athletes.html
This site covers famous Russian athletes.

www.leaguelineup.com/miscinfo.asp?menuid=35&url=russian baseball&sid=5368439
This website offers a look at baseball in Russia.

traveltips.usatoday.com/famous-art-museums-russia-3481.html
Travel Tips lists some famous art museums in Russia.

FESTIVALS

Children from the City Palace of Child and Junior Arts take part in the parade on the annual City Day in Ulan-Ude, Buryatia, Russia.

AFTER THE 1917 REVOLUTION, ALL religious holidays were abolished in the USSR and branded as "vestiges of the past." The old holidays were forcibly replaced by new ones that usually celebrated some aspect of the revolution or the new political dogmas. The people accepted some of these holidays and willingly celebrated them at first, but recent political changes have affected people's attitude towards these festivals.

Revolution Day, for example, was held on November 7. It marked the Bolshevik Revolution of 1917 which overthrew the czar and established a Communist government. This was an official holiday until 2004, when the Russian Parliament removed it from the list of public holidays and replaced it with the older, prerevolutionary Unity Day on November 4.

POLITICAL AND PATRIOTIC HOLIDAYS

DEFENDER OF THE FATHERLAND DAY February 23 is a public holiday throughout Russia, with most schools, banks, and official buildings closed. It marks the achievements of veterans and the military, but is also celebrated as Men's Day.

12

Russian Easter eggs are decorated in a variety of folk art traditions. One style is *pysanky*, which uses a wax resist technique. Other eggs are painted in bright folk designs, and still others are dyed gold and adorned with images of saints and religious symbols.

A Victory Day celebration in 2014 in Moscow

MAY DAY May 1 is Labor Day. Before 1991, the day had a political meaning, commemorating the Day of International Solidarity of Working People. Today, the nature of the May Day celebration has changed and it is now called Spring Holiday.

INTERNATIONAL WOMEN'S DAY In lieu of Mother's Day, Russians celebrate Women's Day on March 8. The celebration was instituted by Clara Zetkin, a veteran German Communist Party leader, as a day of struggle for women's rights. It gradually lost its political content and became Women's Day, on which it was customary for men to present women with flowers and candy, pay them compliments, and do some of the domestic chores around the house.

VICTORY DAY Russia's most popular patriotic holiday is celebrated on May 9—the day hostilities ceased in World War II. Military parades are held in Moscow's Red Square, fireworks are exploded over the city, wreaths are laid at the tombs of those who gave their lives fighting for their country, and surviving veterans are honored. A minute's silence is observed in tribute to those who died defending their country in the two world wars.

RUSSIA DAY June 12 marks the 1990 declaration of Russia as a sovereign state, the first official step taken toward the dissolution of the Soviet Union. It became a public holiday in 1994, but many people—primarily those opposed to the breakup of the USSR— refused to acknowledge it. Originally designated as the Day of Signing the Declaration of State Sovereignty, the occasion was renamed Russia Day in 2002.

UNITY DAY The meaning of this November 4 holiday is somewhat muddled, partly because it's an old commemoration which has only recently been restored. Some people celebrate it as a day of tolerance between the many ethnic and religious groups in Russia. Traditionally, however, it marks an uprising that freed Moscow from Polish—Lithuanian occupation forces in 1612, and commemorates its leaders, Kuzma Minin and Dmitry Pozharsky. For some, November 4 is a religious feast day in the Orthodox Church which celebrates Our Lady of Kazan. Most Russians are simply happy to have a day off, whatever the reason.

TRADITIONAL HOLIDAYS

Russia's most popular holidays have an ancient and traditional origin; many of the celebrations date back to pre-Christian times. They have much in common with festivals celebrated in other parts of Europe.

At the Maslenitsa Festival in Orel, Russia, celebrants burn a Kostroma, or straw effigy of Lady Maslenitsa, to banish winter and welcome spring.

NEW YEAR New Year is celebrated with much vigor and fanfare in Russia and includes a brightly decorated Christmas tree and the exchange of New Year gifts followed by a hearty dinner. According to tradition, an abundant meal signifies an abundant New Year.

CHRISTMAS The New Year's festivities go on all week, culminating in Christmas, which, according to the Orthodox Christian calendar, occurs on January 7. Christmas itself is actually a quieter occasion than the New Year's celebrations, and is observed as a day for family and church.

MASLENITSA A popular winter holiday, Maslenitsa, the equivalent of the religious observance of Shrovetide, is also called Butter Week or Pancake Week in Russia. It begins the day before Ash Wednesday, the first day of Lent in the Christian calendar. Maslenitsa actually predates Christianity and includes some pagan traditions. Festivities last a full week, with snowball fights, masquerades, and sleigh rides among the highlights. People sit down to an elaborate meal because it is traditionally the last chance to feast on rich foods before the fasting period of Lent. The highlight of this holiday is the eating of bliny (BLEE-nee) or pancakes, a symbol of Yarilo, the ancient pagan sun-god. It is also a time to mark the coming of spring, and a straw effigy of Maslenitsa, representing winter, is burned at a carnival.

EASTER This Christian holiday remains a favorite observance in Russia, and to religious people, it is the holiest day of the year. Like many Eastern European countries, Russians celebrate with specially painted Easter eggs with intricate folk art designs. Easter foods include *kulich*, a tall, cylindrical Russian Easter bread with raisins, nuts, and candied fruits, and *pashka*, a molded, sweet white cheese dessert in the shape of a pyramid, decorated with religious symbols.

SABANTUI, SURKHARBAN, AND NAVRUZ Many of Russia's ethnic groups have their own spring holidays that are connected with the completion of the sowing of spring crops. Sabantui is celebrated by the Tatars, and Navruz by other Muslim peoples, but the basic motivation is the same

A Russian Easter bread is surrounded by decorated eggs.

for all—to express joy in anticipation of the coming summer harvest. The name "Sabantui" is thought to have come from an old nomadic tribe called the Saban. The word later came to mean "plough" and "spring crops." The word "tui" means celebration. Hence the word Sabantui has come to mean the festival marking the sowing of spring crops. In the days leading up to Sabantui, farmers make little presents for children, such as painted eggs, sweet cookies, and buns. On the day itself, people compete in various games and activities such as running, wrestling, the three-legged race, the sack race, and an egg-and-spoon race. All are fiercely contested and popular, and provide those watching with an amusing and exciting spectacle.

The Buryats have a similar holiday, Surkharban (Soor-kah-BAHN), that is celebrated in summer after the crops have been sown. Archery competitions are the main event, as well as wrestling and horse racing. Among the Muslims of Asian Russia, the most important festival is Navruz. It is celebrated particularly by the Uzbeks and Tajiks—the peoples of two former Soviet republics. In the towns and villages, people take to the streets to celebrate the arrival of spring by carrying bouquets of flowers and singing songs to honor the blossoming of nature.

INTERNET LINKS

www.timeanddate.com/holidays/russia
This site lists the official and unofficial holidays with links to their background.

rbth.com/arts/2013/05/05/easter_mix_orthodox_ritual_meets_ soviet_custom_25651.html
"Orthodox ritual meets Soviet custom on Easter celebrations" is an article about the way the holiday is celebrated today.

rbth.com/travel/2013/03/09/seven_things_to_do_on_the_seven_ days_of_maslenitsa_23647.html
"Seven things to do on the seven days of Maslenitsa" is a look at how contemporary Russians celebrate this holiday.

FOOD

Stroganina is a traditional Siberian food made of shavings of frozen river fish.

13

I N A COUNTRY THE SIZE OF RUSSIA, which spans so many different regions, and includes people of so many ethnicities, the cuisine is naturally as varied as the land itself. Nevertheless, certain Russian foods are beloved not only nationwide, but around the world as well.

Russians love bread—to them it truly is the staff of life—and the word *khleb* ("bread") is associated in Russian culture with *khlebosolny* ("hospitality"). Interestingly, however, sandwiches are not a part of Russian cuisine.

A traditional black rye bread is typical of hearty Russian breads.

Warm buckwheat kasha is a favorite Russian cereal.

RUSSIAN CUISINE

Russian cuisine has had a long history, stretching back almost fifteen centuries. Because of this, the dishes eaten today are quite different from those of the Russians' distant ancestors. Nevertheless, it is precisely from Russia's long history that the main national dishes originate: rye bread, bliny (pancakes); pies; kasha (KA-sha), which is a kind of gruel made from wheat, rice, or buckwheat; plus other dishes made from vegetables, mushrooms, nuts, and berries.

The Christian Church, which specified a Lenten diet, had a strong influence on Russian cuisine. According to the old church calendar, 192 to 216 days per year were Lenten days (a time when people were allowed to eat only vegetables, mushrooms, and fish, but no meat). Add to this the fact that meat, milk, and eggs were previously something the common people could afford only on major holidays, and it is understandable why Russian traditional cuisine abounds in dishes made from grain (for example, kasha), vegetables (in particular cabbage, carrots, potatoes, onions, turnips, and peas), berries, mushrooms, and herbs prepared in a variety of ways, especially boiled, salted, or baked.

The non-Lenten diet—roasted meat, game, and poultry—was more characteristic of the ruling classes and the gentry and was borrowed mainly from Europe, in particular France, Poland, and Germany. The difference between the diet of the common people and the ruling classes in Russia was always great until the twentieth century. This gap was particularly noticeable in the fifteenth and sixteenth centuries, when the aristocrats indulged in extravagant and ostentatious feasts. For example, at banquets given by the czars, sometimes as many as two hundred dishes would be served.

Everyone who sits down to a Russian meal is traditionally served bread first. Russian bread is very special—it is a favorite with the Slavic peoples—and it is prepared not from ordinary wheat, but from rye. It has a dark color, is soft and spongy in texture, and has a remarkably pleasant flavor. In Russia,

In his historical novel Prince Serebrenni *(1874), Alexei Tolstoy 1817–1875) described an extravagant feast given by Czar Ivan the Terrible in the sixteenth century:*

"A great many servants in velvet coats stood before the Czar, bowed to him, and soon returned, carrying some two hundred fried swans on gold trays. Thus began the dinner … When they had eaten the swans, the servants returned with some three hundred fried peacocks, whose fine tail feathers swayed over every dish. The peacocks were followed by fish, chicken, meat and cheese pies, bliny of all varieties, plus different patties and fritters. While the guests were eating, the servants carried around ladles and goblets of mead … Although they had spent more than four hours at the table, they were only half way through the meal. The Czar's cooks really outdid themselves on that day. The huge fish caught in the Northern Seas aroused special amazement. The silver and gold basins, which had to be carried by several people, were hardly big enough for the fish. The hares in noodles were also delicious and the guests missed neither the quails in garlic sauce nor the larks spiced with onions and saffron. But then at a sign from the table setters, the salt, pepper and vinegar, as well as the meat and fish dishes, were taken off the tables. The servants brought into the chamber a 180-pound sugar Kremlin and put it on the Tsar's table. It was followed by one hundred gilded and painted trees on which, instead of fruits, were hung cakes made from molasses and honey, as well as other sweetmeats…"

Such extravagance, which sounds fantastic today, was possible only at the czar's table. Ivan the Terrible, in particular, enjoyed entertaining his guests with the most extraordinary of luxury meals.

wheat bread is also baked, but the rye bread is considered far superior and a real treat for foreigners who have not been introduced to this culinary delight.

THE RUSSIAN MEAL

Generally, Russian tables are laid out to include a plate of bread, salt, pepper, and mustard. A guest is first served cold appetizers—cold meat, ham, smoked fish, and vegetables. This also includes the typical Russian salted and marinated tomatoes and cucumbers, plus mushrooms, apples, and of course,

A homemade Russian fish soup is a farm-style meal.

wherever possible, red and black caviar. All these typical Russian appetizers are usually washed down with vodka.

Most Russian menus include soups and broths, but the classic opening dish for any meal is *shchi* (sh-chee), a dish that is one thousand years old. This is a vegetable soup in which cabbage (fresh or sour), potatoes, onions, garlic, carrots, roots, and spices are the basic ingredients. Shchi has a unique flavor created by the cabbage brine and other ingredients. Shchi soup is usually served with sour cream. The soup is particularly delicious if eaten with rye bread. The remarkable popularity of this dish is explained by the ready availability of the basic ingredients as well as its good taste.

Ukha (OO-kha) is a hot fish soup prepared from three or four types of fish with potatoes, onions, spices, and herbs added. It is particularly tasty when prepared in the open on the bank of a river where the fish is said to jump into the kettle straight from the water. This kind of soup is referred to as *rybatskayaukha* (ry-BATS-kaya OO-kha), or fisherman's soup.

Russian main courses are also served hot. This is usually a fish or meat dish, boiled or fried, and garnished with vegetables. Most of these dishes do not differ much from those found in central Europe. Purely Russian main courses are kasha, bliny, and a variety of meat and cabbage pies.

Kasha is a thick or soupy dish made from different cereals, which, along with shchi, is another thousand-year-old national favorite. Kasha can be made of peas and ground or whole grains (buckwheat, wheat of different grades, oats, and rice). Kasha may be served as a thin gruel or thickened, and either sweetened, salted, or left unflavored. The method of preparing is very simple and has been tested through the course of centuries; the ingredients are put into boiling water and cooked slowly on a low flame. According to taste, it can be served with sugar, salt, butter, vegetable oil, or gravy.

Bliny are considered the pride of Russian cuisine. This dish has been passed down from the distant pagan past, perhaps from the eighth or ninth century, and resembles pancakes. Bliny require a minimum of flour with a maximum of water or milk, since a very thin batter is needed. Russian bliny are soft, porous, and fluffy, and readily absorb all the melted butter, sour cream, jam, or honey used as toppings.

Bliny with red caviar is a favorite dish.

Pies are another traditional Russian national dish. Russian pies, or pirozhki (pi-ROSH-ki), are comparatively small, elongated, and consist of a filling covered with pastry that is baked in the oven or deep fried in oil. The pastry for the pies may be leavened or unleavened, and the fillings may differ to include cabbage, peas, turnips, carrots, potatoes, spring onions, mushrooms, meat, fish, and even kasha. One variety of pie is known as *kulebyaka* (kool-ee-BYA-ka). These are large pies, and the filling (meat, mushrooms, onions, cabbage and boiled eggs, or kasha) is spread in layers.

There is another large type of pie that covers the entire baking sheet. These pies are open and not covered with pastry—a bit like a pizza—and are topped with jam. They may have pastry latticework on top.

At the end of the meal, dessert consisting of coffee or tea, traditionally served in a glass, is served with candies or spice cakes. The latter are made with honey and spices and covered with sweet syrup. Spice cakes first appeared in Russia sometime around the ninth century, consisting of a mixture of rye flour and honey or the juice of berries. People later began to add spices—cinnamon, cloves, cardamom, and ginger—and this is how the cakes got their name.

Apart from the spice cakes, a variety of jams and preserves are usually offered with tea. Particularly popular are raspberry, strawberry, apple, and pear jams. Russians often add a spoonful of jam or preserves to their tea instead of using sugar to sweeten the flavor. Many a Russian woman prides herself in making excellent jams and preserves.

DRINKS

The national Russian beverages are *kvass* (k-vhas) and *mors* (morhs). Kvass is a beverage that resembles beer, only less bitter and alcoholic; it is usually made from bread and yeast, although other recipes call for barley, malt, raisins, and other ingredients. Mors is made of berry juice diluted with water and slightly fermented.

In times past, there were many meads (alcoholic drinks fermented from honey and water), but they have since mostly disappeared. Of the strong liquors, Russian vodka is known the world over. It is a very potent alcoholic drink.

A tankard of kvass accompanies rye bread.

CUISINE OF THE TATAR AND VOLGA PEOPLES

The dishes of these people are in many respects similar to those of central Asian, and especially Uzbek, cuisine. Typical of this style of cooking are soups of the *shurpa* (shor-PAH) type—made from vegetables, cereals, and fat mutton. Shurpa is prepared with a lot of onions, as well as spices—pepper, coriander, and bay leaf. Also very popular is a soup made with *katyk* (kah-TIHK), which is a sour milk.

Specific to Tatar cuisine are dishes made with horsemeat that has been boiled, dried, and cured. The Tatars are also known for their dessert candies, including *chak-chak* (chak-chak), which are pieces of pastry boiled in honey.

CUISINE OF THE CAUCASUS

The food of this region is a mixture of central Asian, Georgian, and Azerbaijani cuisines. From the Turks and central Asians come the unleavened flat cakes, plus mutton dishes and shurpa soups. From the Georgians come *shashlyks* and brine cheeses, and from the Azerbaijanis, *khalva* (HAHL-vah), a sweet made from nuts and sunflower seeds. The most typical dish here is *khinkal* (kin-KAHL)—thick noodles boiled with mutton and spices, and *chudu* (choo-DOO)—fried pies of meat, cottage cheese, and onion fillings.

CUISINE OF THE NORTH

This cuisine is the most exotic and unusual. In Arctic conditions, the people have devised a special menu consisting of raw meat and fish. For a long time this was considered a sign of barbarity and savagery, but then it was discovered that the people in northern Russia never suffered from beriberi and other vitamin deficiencies, unlike other Russians. It has also been scientifically proven that their cuisine is ideal for arctic conditions.

Raw food can be of three kinds: fresh meat and fish; the fat and blood of an animal (reindeer, seal, or whale); or both of these two frozen together. *Stroganina* (strog-ah-NIN-ah) is a dish that consists of finely sliced meat or fish that is immediately eaten spiced with salt, roots, and berries. Naturally, northern people also like hot dishes—tea, tea with milk, and hot drinks and products made with reindeer milk.

INTERNET LINKS

goeasteurope.about.com/od/russia/a/Russianfood.htm
This site offers an overview of traditional Russian foods.

rbth.com/arts/2014/07/09/monarchs_menu_feasts_fit_for_russian_tsars_and_emperors_38051.html
"Monarchs' menu" is an amusing look at how the Russian royals ate.

rbth.com/russian_kitchen
The Russian Kitchen is a section on the website Russia Beyond the Headlines.

englishrussia.com/tag/raw-food
This site presents a look at the raw foods of Russia's North.

SHCHI (RUSSIAN CABBAGE SOUP)

This recipe is for a basic cabbage soup. One pound of ground beef, crumbled and cooked, can be added with the onions and other vegetables. Shchi is also made with cubed beef. If using that approach, begin by simmering one pound of cut up beef (such as brisket) in the stock for an hour or more until soft, then adding the remaining ingredients.

2 Tbsp butter
2 medium onions, peeled and chopped
1 large carrot, peeled and coarsely grated
1 rib of celery, chopped
1 head of green cabbage, cored and
   shredded
8 cups beef stock, vegetable stock,
   or water
2 bay leaves
salt, pepper to taste
2 or 3 russet potatoes, peeled and
   cut into 1-inch pieces
1 can (14 ounces) diced tomatoes
1 Tbsp caraway seed
sour cream, fresh dill or parsley

Saute onion, celery, and carrot in butter until soft. Add stock or water, bay leaves, salt and pepper. Bring to a boil. Add cabbage, potatoes, tomatoes, and caraway seed; bring back to a boil, cover pan, and lower heat so soup is just simmering. Simmer for about 45 minutes, or until vegetables are soft. Adjust seasoning, discard bay leaves.

Serve in bowls with a dollop of sour cream and a sprinkle of dill or parsley. Rye or pumpernickel bread is a good accompaniment. The soup can be served right away, but improves after a day or two in the refrigerator. Serves six.

SHARLOTKA (RUSSIAN APPLE CAKE)

1 cup flour
1 cup sugar
6 eggs
4 to 6 tart apples, such as Granny Smith, peeled, cored, and sliced
1 tsp vanilla
¾ tsp baking soda
¼ tsp white vinegar
confectioners (powdered) sugar

Preheat oven to 350°F.

Butter a 9-inch springform pan and dust it lightly with flour, or use baking spray.

Arrange apple slices on the bottom of the pan.

In bowl, beat eggs and sugar on high speed for about 2 or 3 minutes, until pale, thick, and fluffy. Lower speed, and mix in vanilla and then flour.

In a very small bowl, quickly mix the baking soda and vinegar, then add them to the batter. Mix batter gently.

Pour the batter mixture over the apples.

Bake for 55—60 minutes. Cool, remove from pan, and sprinkle top with powdered sugar through a sieve.

MAP OF RUSSIA

E   **F**

- ● Capital city
- ● Major town
- ▲ Mountain peak

Height of land (feet)

- over 9000
- 6000 – 9000
- 3000 – 6000
- 1500 – 3000
- 600 – 1500
- 0 – 600

BERING
SEA

Oymyakon ●

Lena

SEA OF
OKHOTSK

Petropavlovsk-
Kamchatskiy

Khabarovsk ●

CHINA

JAPAN

● Vladivostok

Angara (river), C3, D3
Arkhangelsk, B2
Astrakhan, A3

Caucasus Moutains,
 A3
Central Siberian
 Plateau, D2
Chelyabinsk, B3

Don (river), A2—A3

Elbrus, A3

Irkutsk, D3

Kazan, B3
Kemerova, C3
Khabarovsk, F3
Kiev, A2
Kostroma, A2
Krasnovarsk, C3

Lake Baikal, D3
Lena (river), D2—D3,
 E2

Moscow, A2
Murmansk, B1

Nizhniy Novgorod, A2
Novgorod, A2
Novosibirsk, C3

Ob (river), C3
Omsk, C3
Oymyakon, E2

Perm, B3
Petropavlovsk-
 Kamchatskiy, F2
Pskov, A2

Rostov-on-Don, A3
Ryazan, A2

Samara, A3
Saratov, A3
Smolensk, A2
St. Petersburg, A2

Tomsk, C3
Tula, A2
Tver, A2

Ulan Ude, D3
Ulyanovsk, A3
Ural Mountains, B2

Vladimir, A2
Vladivostok F4
Volga (river), A3, B3
Volgograd, A3

West Siberian Plain,
 C2—C3

Yarosavl, A2
Yekaterinburg, B3
Yenisey (river),
 C2—C3, D3

ECONOMIC RUSSIA

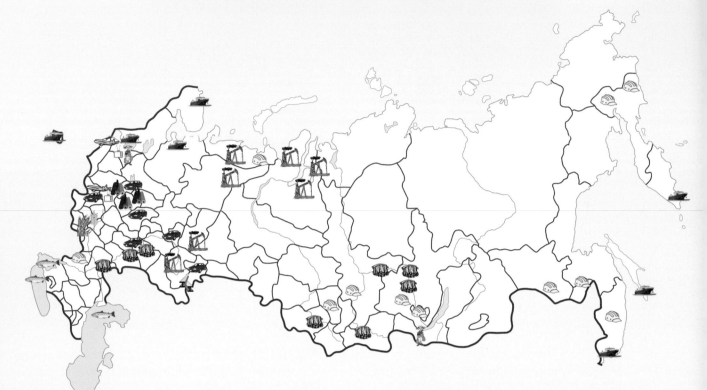

Natural Resources	Manufacturing	Agriculture	Services
Coal	Automobiles	Barley	Airport
Fish	Consumer Goods	Oats	Port
Oil/Natural Gas	Hydroelectricity	Potatoes	Tourism
	Steel	Sunflower Seeds	
	Textiles	Wheat	

OVERVIEW

Russia is a partially reformed economy with a high concentration of wealth in officials' hands. It is a top producer of oil and natural gas and a top exporter of metals such as steel and primary aluminum. Russia's manufacturing sector is generally uncompetitive on world markets and is geared toward domestic consumption. Its economy was hard hit by the 2008—2009 global economic crisis as oil prices plummeted. In 2014, following Russia's military intervention in Ukraine, prospects for economic growth declined further, with expections of zero GDP growth.

GROSS DOMESTIC PRODUCT

$2.553 trillion (2013)
Per capita: $18,100 (2013)

GDP SECTORS

Agriculture 4.2 percent, Industry 37.5 percent, Services 58.3 percent (2013)

AGRICULTURAL PRODUCTS

Beef, fruits, grain, milk, sugar beets, sunflower seed, vegetables

INDUSTRIAL PRODUCTS

Chemicals, coal, construction and farming equipment, durables, electric power generators, foodstuff, gas, handicrafts, machine building, oil, textiles

CURRENCY

1 Russian ruble (RUR) = 100 kopecks
USD 1 ($1) = RUR 63.19
I ruble = $.016 (February 2015)
Notes: 50, 100, 500, 1000 rubles
Coins: 10, 50 kopecks, 1, 2, 5, 10 rubles

NATURAL RESOURCES

Coal, minerals, natural gas, oil, timber

MAJOR TRADE PARTNERS

Belarus, China, France, Germany, Japan, Kazakhstan, Italy, Ukraine, the United States

MAJOR EXPORTS

Chemicals, civilian and military equipment, metals, natural gas, oil, timber, diamonds

MAJOR IMPORTS

Consumer goods, equipment, machinery, meat and poultry, medicine, semifinished metal products, sugar

LABOR FORCE

75.29 million (2013)

LABOR DISTRIBUTION

Agriculture 9.7 percent, Industry 27.8 percent, Services 62.5 percent (2012)

UNEMPLOYMENT RATE

5.8 percent (2013)

INFLATION RATE

6.8 percent (2013)

CULTURAL RUSSIA

Pushkin Festival
Held on the first Sunday in June every year, the Pushkin Festival celebrates the life and works of Russian writer Alexander Pushkin. The festival is held at the Pushkin Estate Museum, located just south of Pskov, and festival goers can expect lectures and poetry readings.

The Hermitage State Museum
One of the greatest and largest museums in the world, the Hermitage in St. Petersburg was once the Winter Palace of Catherine the Great. It is said to house three million exhibits, of which only a fraction can be displayed at any one time.

Mariinsky Theater
This 120-year-old theater in St. Petersburg has played host to the Stars of the White Nights Festival since 1994. In its long history, the theater has seen performances by both the Bolshoi Ballet and the Kirov Opera.

Museum "Vladivostok Fortress"
Opened in 1996, this museum honors the Russian navy and commemorates the three centuries that it has helped to protect the country. Vladivostok has a few other museums with naval themes, which is apt because the town is Russia's easternmost port and currently the home base of the Russian Pacific Fleet.

Ivolginsk Datsan Temple
This temple in Ulan Ude has the largest Buddhist monastery in Russia and is known as the seat of Buddhism in the country.

State Academic Bolshoi Theater
Built in 1776, Moscow's Bolshoi Theater is home to the world-famous Bolshoi Ballet and Bolshoi Opera. It was at this theater that the first production of Tchaikovsky's *Swan Lake* was staged.

Tretiakov Gallery
Located in Moscow, the Tretiakov contains some of the world's most important Russian paintings. One such painting is *Our Lady of Vladimir*, supposedly painted by the apostle Luke.

The Kremlin
Dating back to the twelfth century, the Kremlin in Moscow is known as the seat of the Russian government. The Kremlin is a self-contained city with palaces, cathedrals, armories, and fortresses. Famous sites within the Kremlin include the Red Square, Ivan the Great Belltower, Tsar Cannon and Bell, The Arsenal, Cathedral Square, and the Assumption Cathedral.

OFFICIAL NAME
The Russian Federation

NATIONAL FLAG
Three equal, horizontal bands with white at the top, blue in the middle, and red at the bottom.

NATIONAL ANTHEM
"Gimn Rossiyskoy Federatsii" (Anthem of the Russian Federation)

NATIONAL SYMBOLS
Bear, double-headed eagle

CAPITAL
Moscow

OTHER MAJOR CITIES
Chelyabinsk, Irkutsk, Kazan, Khabarovsk, Kostroma, Magnitogorsk, Nizhniy Novgorod, Novgorod, Novosibirsk, Omsk, Perm, Petropavlovsk-Kamchatskiy, Pskov, Ryazan, Samara, Saratov, Smolensk, St. Petersburg, Tomsk, Tver, Ulyanovsk, Vladimir, Vladivostok, Volgograd, Yaroslavl, Yekaterinberg

POPULATION
142,470,272 (2014)

LIFE EXPECTANCY AT BIRTH
70.16 years (2013)

INFANT MORTALITY RATE
7.08 deaths per 1,000 live births (2013)

ETHNIC GROUPS
Russian 77.7 percent, Tatar 3.7 percent, Ukrainian 1.4 percent, Bashkir 1.1 percent, Chuvash 1 percent, Chechen 1 percent, other 10.2 percent, unspecified 3.9 percent (2010)

RELIGIONS
Russian Orthodox 75 percent, Muslim 6.5 percent, other Christian 2 percent (2008)

LITERACY RATE
99.7 percent

TIMELINE

IN RUSSIA	IN THE WORLD
1200 BCE Cimmerians settle in the area now known as Ukraine	**753** BCE Rome is founded.
	117CE The Roman Empire reaches its greatest extent, under Emperor Trajan.
800 CE Eastern Slavic tribes settle in various regions of Russia.	**600** CE Height of Mayan civilization.
988 CE Grand Prince Vladimir I converts to Christianity and the Eastern Orthodox Church.	**1000** The Chinese perfect gunpowder and begin to use it in warfare.
1240 Mongols rule Russia.	
1547 Ivan IV—Ivan the Terrible—crowned first "czar of all the Russias."	**1530** Beginning of transatlantic slave trade organized by the Portuguese in Africa.
	1558–1603 Reign of Elizabeth I of England
	1620 Pilgrims sail the *Mayflower* to America.
1682 Peter the Great becomes czar and begins modernizing Russia.	**1776** US Declaration of Independence signed.
	1789–1799 The French Revolution
1825 The Decembrists stage a revolt in St. Petersburg. The revolt fails.	**1861** The US Civil War begins.
	1869 The Suez Canal is opened.
1905 Revolution forces Nicholas II to create State Duma.	**1914** World War I begins.
1917 Revolutionaries overthrow the Russian government.	
1922 The Union of Soviet Socialist Republic (USSR) is formed.	

IN RUSSIA	IN THE WORLD
1930 Joseph Stalin begins reign of terror.	
	1939 World War II begins.
	1945 World War II ends.
1948 The Soviet Union cuts off contact with the Western world starting the Cold War.	**1949** The North Atlantic Treaty Organization (NATO) is formed.
	1957 The Russians launch *Sputnik*.
	1966–1969 The Chinese Cultural Revolution
	1986 Nuclear power disaster at Chernobyl in Ukraine
1991 The USSR collapses and President Gorbachev resigns.	
2000 Vladimir Putin elected president.	**1997** Hong Kong is returned to China.
	2001 Terrorists crash planes in New York, Washington, DC, and Pennsylvania.
2004 Russia invades Georgia; Putin wins second term	**2003** War in Iraq
	2005 London hit by terrorist bombings
2008 Putin becomes prime minister	**2008** Barack Obama elected US president
	2010 Massive earthquakes devastate Haiti and Chile
2012 Russian forces take over Crimea	**2011** "Arab Spring" movement topples governments in the Middle East
	2013 Nelson Mandela dies at age ninety-five.
2014 Pro-Russian rebels revolt against Ukrainian government.	**2014** ISIS terrorists take over large parts of Syria and Iraq.

GLOSSARY

Cyrillic alphabet
A written system developed in the ninth century for Slavic peoples of the Eastern Orthodox faith.

bliny (BLEE-ny)
Light, porous, fluffy pancakes that combine the the minimum amount of flour with the maximum amount of water or milk.

Duma (DOO-ma)
The state assembly or council that was first initiated as a result of the failed 1905 Revolution.

glasnost (GLAS-nost)
Former USSR president Mikhail Gorbachev's declared public policy of openly discussing economic and political realities. Literally means "openness."

kasha (KA-sha)
A dish made from a variety of cereals.

Kremlin
A fortress in medieval Russian cities. The Moscow Kremlin is used as the seat of Russian government. The term "Kremlin" is often used to signify the Russian government itself.

pirozhki (pi-ROSH-ki)
Small elongated pies that are baked in the oven or deep fried in oil.

serfs
Peasants bound by oath to a hereditary plot of land and to a landowner in a modified form of slavery. The landowner, in effect, owned the peasants and could buy and sell them as he pleased, or volunteer them for army service.

steppe
A geographic region of extensive flat grasslands, found in the southern and eastern European, western Russia, and southwest Asian parts of Russia.

taiga (TIE-ga)
Coniferous evergreen forests of subarctic lands covering vast tracts of Russia, especially in Siberia.

tundra
One of the vast, nearly level, treeless plains of the arctic regions of Europe and Asia.

FOR FURTHER INFORMATION

BOOKS

Afanasyev, Alexander. *Russian Fairy Tales (Illustrated)*. Melbourne, Australia: The Planet, 2012.

Ascher, Abraham. *Russia, a Short History*. London, England: One World Publications, 2009.

Berdy, Michele. *The Russian Word's Worth: A Humorous and Informative Guide to Russian Language Culture and Translation*. New Russian Writing. Moscow: GLAS New Russian Writing, 2011.

Berge, Ann and Jeff Yesh. *Russia ABCs: A Book About the People and Places of Russia*. Country ABCs. North Mankato, MN.: Capstone Publishing, 2004.

Dorling Kindersley. *DK Eyewitness Travel Guide: Russia*. New York: Dorling Kindersley, 2013.

Figes, Orlando. *Natasha's Dance: A Cultural History of Russia*. New York: Picador, 2003.

Gessen, Masha. *The Man Without a Face: the Unlikely Rise of Vladimir Putin*. London, England: Riverhead Books, 2013.

Kort, Michael. *A Brief History of Russia*. New York: Checkmark Books, 2008.

Malikov, Oleg. *Clash of Cultures: Russia vs. USA or Understanding Russians Inside Out*. Kindle Edition. New York: Amazon.com, 2015.

Solzhenitsyn, Alexander, *One Day in the Life of Ivan Denisovich*. New York: Important Books, 2013.

WEBSITES

CIA World Factbook (select "Russia" from the country list). www.CIA/gov/cia/publications/factbook

Embassy of the Russian Federation in Washington D.C., USA. www.russianembassy.org

President of Russia. eng.kremlin.ru

WayToRussia.Net. www.waytorussia.net

Complete List of Russian Newspapers and Magazine sites in English. www.world-newspapers.com/russia.html

MUSIC

Most Beautiful Folk Songs of Russia, ARC Music, 2009.

Russian Ballet Music, Warner Classics, 2013.

Moscow Nights: Popular Russian Hits, Monitor Records, 2012.

BIBLIOGRAPHY

BBC News, Crimea Profile
www.bbc.com/news/world-europe-18287223

BBC News, Russia Profile/timeline
www.bbc.com/news/world-europe-17840446

Biography.com, "Joseph Stalin Biography."
www.biography.com/people/joseph-stalin-9491723

Biography.com, "Vladimir Putin Biography"
www.biography.com/people/vladimir-putin-9448807

CNN, "2008 Georgia Russia Conflict Fast Facts" March 16, 2014
www.cnn.com/2014/03/13/world/europe/2008-georgia-russia-conflict

GeoCurrents, "Introduction to Siberia"
www.geocurrents.info/place/russia-ukraine-and-caucasus/siberia/introduction-to-siberia

Gordon, Michael R., and David M. Herszenhorn. "U.S. and Europe Working to End Ukraine Fighting." *The New York Times*, February 5, 2015
www.nytimes.com/2015/02/06/world/europe/kerry-biden-hollande-merkel-ukraine-conflict.html?ref=todayspaper&_r=1

MacFarquhar, Neil. "Russia Outlines Prescription to Bolster Its Ailing Economy, but Experts Scoff." *New York Times*, February 2, 2015
www.nytimes.com/2015/02/03/world/europe/russia-details-plans-to-bolster-its-economy-but-experts-scoff.html?ref=todayspaper&_r=0

Nazdracheva, Lyudmila. "Divorce, Russian style." *Russia Beyond the Headlines,* October 16, 2013.
rbth.com/society/2013/10/16/divorce_russian_style_30845.html

Trivedi, Bijal P. "Life Is a Chilling Challenge in Subzero Siberia." *National Geographic News,* May 12, 2004. news.nationalgeographic.com/news/2004/05/0512_040512_tvoymyakon.html

INDEX

INDEX